D0724644

2005

Small Business, Big Profit!

PEARSON
Prentice Hall
BUSINESS

Books that make you better

Books that make you better – that make you *be* better, *do* better, *feel* better. Whether you want to upgrade your personal skills or change your job, whether you want to improve your managerial style, become a more powerful communicator, or be stimulated and inspired as you work.

Prentice Hall Business is leading the field with a new breed of skills, careers and development books. Books that are a cut above the mainstream – in topic, content and delivery – with an edge and verve that will make you better, with less effort.

Books that are as sharp and smart as you are.

Prentice Hall Business.
We work harder – so you don't have to.

For more details on products, and to contact us, visit
www.pearsoned.co.uk

NICK RAMPLEY-STURGEON

Small Business, Big Profit!

How to increase the profitability of your entrepreneurial business

Harlow, England • London • New York • Boston • San Francisco • Toronto • Sydney • Singapore • Hong Kong
Tokyo • Seoul • Taipei • New Delhi • Cape Town • Madrid • Mexico City • Amsterdam • Munich • Paris • Milan

PEARSON EDUCATION LIMITED

Edinburgh Gate
Harlow CM20 2JE
Tel: +44 (0)1279 623623
Fax: +44 (0)1279 431059
Website: www.pearsoned.co.uk

First published in Great Britain in 2006

ISBN-13: 978-0-273-67519-8
ISBN-10: 0-273-67519-2

British Library Cataloguing in Publication Data
A catalogue record for this book is available from the British Library

Library of Congress Cataloging-in-Publication Data
Rampley-Sturgeon, Nick.
  Small business, big profit! : how to increase the profitability of your
entrepreneurial business / Nick Rampley-Sturgeon.
    p. cm.
  Includes index.
  ISBN-13: 978-0-273-67519-8 (alk. paper)
  ISBN-10: 0-273-67519-2
    1. Small business—Management. 2. Corporate profits. I. Title.

  HD62.7.R36 2005
  658.4'012—dc22

                                                             2005051344

10 9 8 7 6 5 4 3 2 1
09 08 07 06 05

Typeset in 9.5pt Iowan by 70
Printed and bound in Great Britain by Henry Ling Ltd, Dorchester

The Publisher's policy is to use paper manufactured from sustainable forests.

Contents

Preface

If you are starting or running a business, or thinking about it, you're in good company. And you really matter. After all, small business **IS** business. Since the majority of businesses in the UK, or in any country in the world, are ventures comprising no more than half a dozen people, it is clear that small business is **the** force that runs economies, funds taxation systems and provides employment for the majority of the populace.

Over 60% of all UK businesses have no staff. They are one-person operations or husband and wife outfits, with an average total turnover of just below £60,000 a year. This group represents over 2.5 million businesses and households out of the 3.8 million businesses registered in the UK. Of the 1.2 million businesses that employ staff, nearly 800,000 have four staff or less and around 200,000 have nine staff or less.

Running a business can be lucrative, enjoyable and a great way to earn a living and create wealth. However, many small-business owners find life a struggle at some time or other. If frustrated by their lack of financial success, some may even question why they went into business in the first place.

Whether you are enjoying the experience but simply want to make it all more profitable, or whether you are finding it all a bit trying and are looking for ways to bring more profit and more fulfilment into your business, this book is full of advice, tips and techniques that will help. And if you are just setting out on your first business venture, and are eager to ensure that you make your enterprise profitable from the start, then you'll find plenty of guidance here too.

This book is for you if:

- you are running a business that you think could generate more profit
- you want to grow or refine your business but are not sure which way to go
- you find your cash flow doesn't run quite as it should

- you are finding your business is too much of a struggle and does not deliver enough profit . . . or pleasure
- you are thinking of starting a business and want to ensure you maximize the profit potential from day one
- your family has a business that you want to help improve
- you are looking for new ideas to improve your business (be it sales, marketing, products, services, finance).

Throughout the book we refer to clients and customers. For some people, each word implies a distinct group – 'customer' implying those in a shop environment and 'client' people in an exclusively professional environment. Both terms are used in this book, but not to imply one group of people rather than another.

Whatever your fears, frustrations or concerns, during the course of this book we will review every aspect of running a business that can affect its success, and especially profit. Even taking just one idea from each chapter will help you to evaluate the scope for shift and change so that you can implement it in your own venture. There are new opportunities all around you. You simply have to adopt new thinking and new behaviours in order to grab those opportunities.

Running a small business is often a lifestyle choice, it is not always just about money. It can be a very satisfying, as well as fruitful, way to live. This book will help you enjoy your business more and it could improve your bank balance at the same time.

I have been self-employed and running businesses for more than fifteen years. In that time I have sat down with thousands of small-business owners just like myself and looked at ways they can grow, change and prosper. This desire to find a better way has never left me. As a business owner I know what it is like to struggle with the gap between effort and reward, originality and branding, cash flow and profit. Even today, with activities centring on three areas – mail order, business education and business development – we remain essentially a small business. We employ several full-time staff in our ventures and rely on the availability of others who can help us on a temporary basis when we have a big project or a new information launch.

Small business **IS** business. Yours and mine.

If you currently feel you are lacking a sense of direction, I hope this book and the ideas it contains will give you a clearer focus. Where what you do now seems endlessly repetitive or exhausting, I want to share ideas that will remind you of the potential you first saw in your business and get you excited about your venture once more. You have great offerings for the world, but perhaps lack the understanding of how best to exploit them and bring them to market. If you are tired of the ongoing and daily grind of big routine for little reward, I can suggest ideas for creating new revenue streams and steer you gently in the direction of higher and stronger profits.

You already know most of what you would like to change about your existing business. I passionately believe that this book will give you the processes and the techniques that you require to make the changes and get the results you so dearly want.

Remember that you are in business because you choose to be. Remember also that it is your choice each day to continue with your business and to continue to strive to improve it. Your business may be small, but there is absolutely no reason why it should not deliver healthy and juicy *Big Profits!* It's your business, your choice and your future.

Nick Rampley-Sturgeon
2005

Author's acknowledgements

With grateful thanks to the many individuals who showed kindness and great patience in sharing with me details of the way they run their businesses. In each question they showed enthusiasm for the project and demonstrated their own hunger to see a book that would help other business owners like themselves create more sustainable ventures.

A particular thank you to my friends William Barron, Keith Banfield, Frank Furness, and Alastair Kennedy for their support and encouragement in differing ways over the years. Their constant belief has always been greatly valued.

Others who need special mention are Jane Moseley and Jackie Strachan of JMS Books for their inspired editorial work. And always somewhere in the background, Rachael Stock, my editor at Pearson Education for taking me through the creative process from the initial first ideas meeting to the finished product now in your hands.

Most importantly of all, thank you to my family, Joanna, Henry and Johnny, for your love, support and understanding in allowing me to get on with the book after already busy days. Thanks for letting me chase another idea, interview or product concept that may have made little sense then. I hope it does now. Thanks boys for constantly displaying your own enterprise and for always posing intriguing questions to Daddy!

Publisher's acknowledgements

Figures 3.1, 3.2, 3.3 and 3.5 are adapted with permission from Figures 3.1–3.4 which appear in *Buying to Rent* by Nick Rampley-Sturgeon, FT Prentice Hall, 2002.

CHAPTER ONE

Where are you now?

What are you in this for?

'A BUSINESS OF MY OWN!' has long been the cry of the frustrated employee. It signifies the opportunity to be in the driving seat and to take responsibility for your future. Yet, in reality, the chance to be self-employed is a step which many do not take, fearing the stress and exposure to risk and lack of security that comes from an irregular income, no sick pay or company pension, particularly when there is a family to support.

Independent business ownership is a powerful way forward. Figures from governments around the world show that those who run small businesses are more likely to achieve financial security for themselves and their families over the course of their working lives, than the millions who are part of the conventional, salaried rat race. Employees' salaries are taxed relentlessly and are drained further by contributions to welfare and state pensions.

It is now easier than ever before to create a respectable income from self-employment. A business can be started alongside an existing career or can be a new launch in its own right. In the same way, you can set up and manage new income streams alongside the business you already run. More than this, you can create not just a profitable business, but a lifestyle that supports and nourishes you emotionally. Why not strive for both financial rewards and personal satisfaction?

What about you?

It is very likely that you already own and run your own venture. However, you may not yet have hit the vein of gold that you had hoped to tap when you first began trading, perhaps several months or even several years ago. My mission is to help you change that.

I'm going to make the assumption that you have a business and are trading, but that you know you have only scratched the surface of your potential achievements. If you are considering the first step into business ownership, full-time or perhaps part-time, then there's plenty here to help you make sure you set off in the right way and consider all the issues that will affect your profitability from the outset.

After all, small-business ownership without just reward is no better than the employment trap. One of the reasons you might have picked this book up is because your existing venture is not producing the results you had hoped for. Does it drain your energy, leaving you with little to spare for the family when you eventually get home? Do you work all your waking hours, yet despite this are scared to call the bank to confirm your balance? Perhaps you have additional worries, fearing as you drive to work each day that the premises might have been broken into, the stock stolen or that some staff will be absent.

Know what drives you

In order to take the first step on the road to increased profitability and enjoyment of your business, you need to indulge in a little navel gazing and find out what motivates you. Are you in business because you had a great idea? Or perhaps you wanted to get out of the rat race or desired more control. Or did you simply want to achieve a better future for your family? Truthfully assessing your current situation and identifying what drives you, will help you go forward in the right way and, for some, plan the changes that you need to make to put an end to the stagnation, stress and discontent of having an unprofitable business. Once you have identified what is wrong, you can take steps to rectify it. And once you have clarified your motivation, you can make sure the steps you take will suit your outlook on life.

Entrepreneurs are widely admired as role models (Richard Branson, James Dyson, Donald Trump even). All these people employ large numbers of staff, but have managed to promote themselves primarily because they have a message of enterprise and perseverance in the face of the mega corporations. Many thousands of small business owners are, in their own way, just as successful and important – the quiet, unacknowledged stars of their local business communities. Whether they employ just three or four staff, or as many as twenty, each employee receiving a wage is being paid by small-scale private enterprise, and the money goes back into the economy for the wider good.

Think about who your original role models were, both those in the public eye and out of it.

Wherever we go, our high streets and shopping malls are dominated by the same branded chain stores. Yet you and I look to small businesses to fix our cars, decorate our homes, sell us flowers or deliver pizza. Some fall by the wayside, but many enjoy longevity and local newspapers often carry stories of small businesses celebrating their tenth, twentieth or thirtieth anniversaries. Small business makes up the business community in your neighbourhood. Attend a local chamber of commerce or other business group meeting and you will encounter owners and managers of all kinds of businesses, from one-person outfits to firms with fifteen local staff, but almost all will be small ventures.

Which were the local businesses that inspired you? Which ones made you think, 'I want to be like them'?

Understanding your beginnings

Maybe you started out working for a big corporate. Perhaps you went straight into the family business. You may have even gone straight from school or college into working for yourself. Spend a bit of time now thinking about your route to where you are today.

CASE IN POINT

My formative influences about running a business began in Latin America, where I spent over a year, as part of my degree. I was constantly impressed by the resourcefulness and courage of families who had to survive in an environment with no state support infrastructure. I lived in a poor, border village high in the mountains between Mexico and Guatemala. The whole community was dedicated to and dependent upon trading for its survival. Not standard market trading but a more traditional kind, peddling pots, cutlery, knives, candles, blankets, and more. Each week the menfolk left the village carrying as much as they could in roughly-woven cloth backpacks that towered above their heads. After days spent walking between the mountain communities they returned home, the simple sign of success being that their backpacks had shrunk, their contents sold on.

After college I moved into corporate employment, managing only five years as a 'salary man' before I could stand it no longer and had to go my own way. But those five years were with two international giants, one at the top of the global computer industry and the other in international finance.

Big corporate life might seem at first sight a false start on the road to self-employment. However, skills learned under the corporate umbrella – the ability to communicate effectively with small teams, the use of systems and the value of structure – can be applied very effectively to *Small Business, Big Profit!* scenarios.

To take full advantage of opportunities and plan for the future, take a little time out now to look at how you got into business and what keeps you there.

What's your story?

Take a look at the following questions and answer them in the light of your own experience. Something or someone triggered your curiosity and got you thinking about the possibilities, problems, challenges and benefits of running your own venture. Awareness and understanding of your business-related aspirations will come from an insight into who or what has influenced you so far. Someone within your family, school or work community had a greater influence on you than others on the value and merits of working for yourself, creating opportunity, building an income.

- Who were your first business-owning role models?
- What examples did you see of family-run businesses?
- How well did they do financially?
- What was good, bad or unique about them?
- How was commerce or business covered at school?
- What about at home?
- Were there any self-employed people within your extended family?
- What involvement did you have with small businesses in the community?
- What triggered your wanting to get into a business of your own?
- Who are the business owners and small entrepreneurs you admire?
- Why these people?
- Did anything they do impress you particularly and act as a catalyst for you?
- What have you learned from them that has value for you?

If you decided to skip the previous questions and came straight to this paragraph to save some time, then please go back to the beginning. I listed these questions because they are of value. Taking a considered and strategic approach to what got you into business in the first place, will help you apply the same approach to your future direction.

What do you think of it so far?

How do you feel your business is doing and how does it compare with your original vision?

- When you started your business, what dreams did you have in your mind for yourself?
- How do those dreams stack up now compared with what you have created so far?
- Does the thought of where you are now fill you with pride, satisfaction and enthusiasm?
- Are you embarrassed by how little has changed in the five months or even five years since the launch of your venture?
- In your own mind, how do you feel you have done?
- What do you feel you should have achieved to date?
- What happened to the original game plan?

What keeps you going?

Each of us has our own set of personal ethics, which I will call our 'guiding principles'. These are the things that matter to us in life, the principles that form the personal creed by which we live. They influence the way we behave in our relationships, underpinning all our time and life management issues, and so naturally affect our business lives too.

We place value on virtues such as trust, honesty, friendship and love. For some, their guiding star is the importance of their family, achieving financial security, or making a contribution to the community. For others, it is the accumulation of knowledge and expertise, or leaving a healthy legacy.

To establish your guiding principles, ask yourself these two fundamental questions and jot down the answers:

1 What are the most important things in my life?
2 Of these, which do I value the most?

If you are having trouble getting started, here are a few suggestions to help you. They are not in any particular order since everyone has a different ranking of such important issues.

- Spouse or partner and family
- Financial security, or even to become wealthy
- A sense of achievement and work satisfaction
- Quality of life
- Integrity and ethics
- Education and learning
- Service for the common good – providing employment
- The need to keep active and stimulated
- Independence and being in control

Now review the extent to which your daily life, on both a personal and business level, incorporates these ideals and higher principles successfully. Do they play less of a part in your daily life than you would like? If so, it may be an uncomfortable realization – but you can take heart from the fact that you are not alone. Many people find marrying the needs of the business

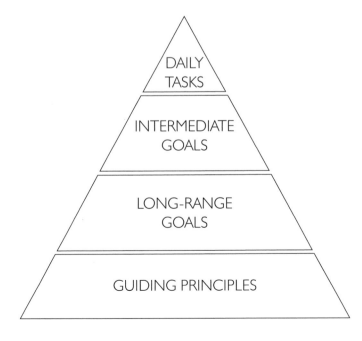

with their higher principles extremely difficult. But are the two resolutely incompatible? The drive to lead a life that is meaningful, and which provides satisfaction and fulfilment on a personal level, need not be completely at odds with the need to support a family, look after financial requirements and work comfortably with other people.

The key is awareness. Once you have established what is important to you, it will be easier to incorporate your higher values into your daily life. Unless you live a serene and blameless life on a par with a minor eastern deity, you won't be able to achieve perfection; but simply striving to live your day-to-day life steered by your guiding principles can provide a degree of satisfaction in itself.

Applying your guiding principles to business

To apply your guiding principles in your professional life, write down some positive statements about your business. These may be goals that you have already achieved, while others may still be aspirational, such as:

- My business contributes strongly to the local economy.
- I am a good financial manager and a shrewd investor.
- I am a good employer.
- My employment of local people supports the community.
- My business enjoys strong cash flow and regular income streams.
- It is our company policy to provide an environment for learning.

You can then break down these statements into their underlying values and how they relate to your situation.

For example, if your value is 'Being a good employer', then you might write:

- I am careful about what promises I make to staff.
- I use ethically-produced products.
- I contribute to staff development and training.
- I monitor the win–win value of our supplier relationships.
- I am maintaining my involvement in community issues.

If your value is 'Being a good financial manager and a shrewd investor', then the pointers may be:

- I save 20% of all revenue for tax provision.
- All my acquisitions are profitable.
- I have developed several sources of income.
- I reward my staff with financial and benefits incentives.
- I am increasing my understanding of small-business funding.

Investing time and effort in writing down and then reviewing your guiding principles forces you to think deeply about your priorities so that you can align your behaviour with your beliefs. The result will provide you with a mission statement that can be applied in your business life, leading to a greater sense of personal fulfilment. When times are stressful and uncertain, it will be at hand to assist you in decision-making and put you back on track. There will be a sense of vision about what you do. Rather than reacting to and being governed by the events around you, you will begin to take control. And with the simple act of writing down these principles you will begin to think of the actions you can take to move closer to the achievement of your goals.

My own guiding principles have strengthened and become more focused over the years. They are now just one sentence long, but this one sentence keeps me on track.

Where do I go from here?

You should now have clarified why you are in business, assessed your progress to date and clarified what higher principles are important to you. You might have thought that these things were obvious, but have found them not to be so simple after all. On the other hand, perhaps it has been crystal clear to you all along. Whatever the outcome, by having identified clearly where you are now and what motivates you, you have laid the groundwork for the next step – thinking about strategy and where you go from here.

CHAPTER TWO

Strategic planning

Building a business on lasting foundations

How do you envisage your business looking in three to five years' time? Do you intend to sell it? Grow it? Take on new staff to free up your time? Diversify? If you want to improve profitability, move on and achieve great things for your company, a clearly defined strategy is a must.

A strategy is for life!

Strategic action plans are about transforming your vision into a strong reality. Armed with the new awareness and understanding of your motivating forces and personal values that you have gained from working through Chapter 1, you can now set about working out your *Big Profit!* strategy.

Strategic planning involves both the means and the end. The means is your plan, the action that you will take to make your vision reality, and the end is your goal, your vision for your business. By their very nature, strategic planning and management are worthless if they are not visionary.

A strategy is important because:

- Your *Small Business, Big Profit!* venture will get nowhere without one: a rudderless business without a direction will flounder without focus and purpose.

- Knowing where you are going and the path you will take to get there means that more time can be spent on the issues and activities that will lead to increased profitability. Its time-saving benefits affect all aspects of business. Less time is wasted in discussions, making decisions or being distracted by the side issues.

- It helps reduce mistakes, which means saving the time that would normally be spent on rectifying them, and the business keeps on track. When the business is on track, it stands a better chance of making a steady profit. Sporadic deals made on the hoof without following a game plan might generate big profits, but since these profits are sporadic too, they will be whittled away during quiet periods. Coupled with their uncertain nature, sporadic deals are not a recipe for long-term success. Planning for steady profit is the way forward to that continual *Big Profit!* goal.

- It will also help you shape your business to keep abreast of market trends. Plan to acquire new skills, invest in new equipment, software or staff training in order not to be left behind by the new guys in town. With a strategy, the unknown soon becomes the familiar and change can be more easily accepted, implemented and even welcomed.

A well-thought-out strategy will set you on the path towards gaining the benefits and reaping the financial rewards that you originally went into business to achieve.

Too often businesses focus on the 'here and now', on the transactions and activities of every day, taking their eyes off their goal, the vision of what the business could become. Keep focused on what you are looking to achieve and don't let the day-to-day matters and events distract you.

Developing your strategy need not be as difficult as you might imagine. You need to ask yourself some simple questions:

- Where am I starting from?
- Where do I want to go?
- What is my route or journey plan?
- How do I stay on course and track my progress?

A basic principle for translating your business vision into a living reality is to look at your driving goal. An effective strategy will deliver the vision you have of the business, but you can achieve this only through the creation of mini action plans.

Think about the four questions above and see these now as being broken down into some key steps:

- Identify the goals to be achieved and the timescale to be applied.
- Agree what you are achieving currently (your benchmark).
- Set clear strategic objectives.
- Establish what indicators you will use to monitor and judge the achievement of those objectives.
- Identify the obstacles and issues you will need to overcome to achieve the objectives.
- Establish the key milestones that will show you are making progress towards the main goal.

Know where you are going

The more time you spend in working out your strategy, the greater your chances of achieving your long-term goals.

Imagine you are going on a trip. You decide on your destination and set off early one morning. At the end of the day, having travelled at a reasonable pace, you reach your final destination. So what was it that made your trip successful? Probably having a clear idea of where you were going, a well-thought-out route, with a few judiciously timed rest stops along the way.

What's your destination? What do you want to achieve? A good place to start is to work out what income you need to live the kind of life you want after having made deductions for bills and taxes. Whether your goal is to make £60,000 from a home-based mail order operation, or €80,000 from an Internet download service, you need to identify what kind of turnover it is reasonable to seek from such a venture. Will it be sufficient to give you the income you want? If not, you need to think again.

Work out how you will get there

How are you are going to achieve the turnover you want? Begin by asking yourself a few questions such as: How can the business attract revenue throughout the year? What scope is there is for adding new revenue streams? How might you increase the volume of trade? What will be the impact upon your diary, personal life, stress levels, bank finances, etc.

To attempt to take your existing business in a new direction without investing sufficient time to plan and think things through would be very foolish and you could find yourself way off track a year or two down the line.

CASE IN POINT

The owners of a coach company with a fleet of 20 vehicles and 47 employees collectively felt that they should be achieving more, and so an outside facilitator was brought in to take them through a strategic planning meeting for the first time. It had been decided not to ask the managing director to do this, since, as a member of the family that owned the company, it might be difficult for him not to give too much weight to their views.

The facilitator helped the company to clarify their understanding of the immediate competition and encouraged them to look beyond the local area at other businesses delivering similar or related services, asking them to question how they wanted their venture to be perceived.

As a result, they decided upon a strategy for moving from where they were to where they wanted to be that involved three elements:

- **Competition awareness**, using their current position as a benchmark for progress.
- **Staff involvement** in both implementing the strategy and managing the change.
- **Specific action plans** created within each of these areas.

In a different scenario, a large city museum was instructed by its local authority to put the vacant part of its premises to good use by providing entertainment and leisure facilities from which revenues could be earned.

In this case, a primary component of the museum's development strategy was market research, since they were looking at developing a new aspect of their existing operation. They decided to canvass local organizations, businesses and networks to identify how those groups currently selected meeting and exhibition space and party venues. The issue of staff involvement became another component, along with a new approach to public relations (PR) and marketing.

In common with the example of the coach company, however, action plans were needed in each area in order to implement the strategy of becoming a space provider.

Essential strategy components to consider

Essential to the adoption and implementation of strategic actions in your business, is the consideration of the different ways you could lead and develop the venture.

Here are a few ideas to consider.

Leveraging your knowledge

'Leveraging' your knowledge is all about capitalizing on your own intellectual property and getting the most from it. You may think you don't have anything worth selling, but you would be wrong. We all have knowledge and experience of something.

> **CASE IN POINT**
>
> Mark and Jason have worked together for several years as Microsoft engineers within larger corporate structures, but each felt there was something they wanted to do in terms of expressing their technical skills with more of a spirit of enterprise.
>
> By leveraging their IT skills and their love of the Internet as a search engine they developed a Local Search tool that has been applied to websites they now control and which provide database services to five countries. Subscription membership services have provided their business with a strong cash flow and the scope for greater reinvestment into staff training and business growth.
>
> They employ several support staff and continue to grow and develop their business through the fresh application of the knowledge they gained as IT engineers.

What about you? You are an expert in something. Recognizing what that something is and working with it can make a big difference to your *Small Business, Big Profit!* venture. Refusing to do so will inevitably put you under pressure from your competitors.

Install structures for passive and repeat income

Both of these can provide the *Small Business* owner with ample opportunity to secure some *Big Profit!* with minimal or even no effort. Don't miss out on these opportunities to add to your bottom line. See Chapter 4 where these are explained in detail.

Get out of your own way

If you are happy enough to stay in the launch phase of your business, the surest way of doing so is by continuing to shoulder the whole workload yourself. To get the business moving faster, you need to look seriously at employing staff and developing teams of people who can both replicate you and take on far more besides. Recognize your own and others' strengths and weaknesses and hire accordingly.

In order to expand, think about developing your venture in a similar way to a 'franchise'. You don't need to go down the path of actually buying into a franchise, but you do need to recognize the strain on your time and consider employing people who can do some of the work you have been doing.

Diversify within your area of specialization to spread your risk

Part of your strategy must include reviewing the spread of your business interests. When starting out, it is better to focus on one core activity, but once your business is well established and in good condition financially, you can investigate moving into related business areas. Apart from the additional revenue that this can produce, it reduces your dependence upon one area of activity. If the market for your main activity takes a dip, you should still have revenue coming in from other areas.

CASE IN POINT

Pure Flow is a great example of a water engineering business with operations around the world, but which grew from an individual consultant. Now a limited partnership structure with eleven consultants and half a dozen support staff, they provide crisis management solutions to cities or regions experiencing pollution and contamination of water supplies.

Recognizing their dependence upon being contacted for a service in a crisis, they brainstormed over several months to develop a new business model. The strategies that came from this were:

● the development of varied fee-earning services
● the creation of film and audio material that could be sold to potential clients of their crisis support work, ensuring these

> people had been contacted in advance of any potential call on their services
> - the scope to develop risk-management products and services that did not involve water issues.
>
> By analyzing their existing products and services they were able to create fresh opportunities for themselves, and in so doing, diversify through their deliberate strategy of building new revenues.

What about you? To make the most of the areas into which you can diversify, think about which client group is most likely to be the audience for your products or services. How can you go about finding and contacting them?

Learn to say 'no'

Recently, I asked a husband and wife team what they wanted to do in terms of growing their business. They answered, 'Anything people will pay us for, of course!', clearly feeling that the answer was obvious. But this approach can lead to problems. Don't spread your services and options so wide that you will travel anywhere to service any customer for almost any price – you will almost certainly lose out to companies who take a more professional and focused approach.

Managing change in your business

As a small business owner, you may not have had experience of implementing strategic goals before or thought about how to manage change either. With change comes the inevitable risk of encountering resistance from staff, suppliers and your business agents. Such challenges or 'blockers' to progress can be a real headache. In order to ease the path for change, look at improving communication within the business to help staff understand the benefits that the new active strategies will bring for them. To accept the new vision and strategy, people will need to believe that it will benefit them. Such benefits can be seen in terms of better opportunities for the business, reflected through more revenues, enhanced employment prospects, greater staff benefits, and so forth.

To minimize the initial negative reactions that can follow the introduction of change, try looking at a certain aspect of your business and identifying some process or operation that it is generally acknowledged could be improved upon. Form a working group or 'strategy task force' to assess the process as it is currently, envision the improvement and identify the blockers that are impeding it. Ask the task force to find the solutions or 'enablers' required to achieve a successful outcome.

The ethics of win–win

The way you go about making your business a success, in the ethical sense, is another component of your strategy. Almost all of us want the best for our families, our staff and our clients. We expect a fair reward for our effort. We are conscious that in order to secure clients who will return to us again and again, we have to behave in a certain way. We also understand that once we have attracted the right calibre of staff to operate and manage the business, the last thing we should do is lose them and have to start again.

Ethical trading and building good relationships as a result can also form part of your *Big Profit!* strategy.

'I'm all right, Jack'

However, not all business owners have the same approach, and, because of this, I suspect that they comprise a fair proportion of those who are struggling. Many business owners behave as though they and their families are the only people who matter. As a result they pay their staff as little as they can get away with and certainly don't waste any money on foolish 'luxuries' such as education, training, welfare and bonuses. Nor are they straight in their dealings with clients but are always on the lookout for a better offer, regardless of ethical concerns.

> ### CASE IN POINT
>
> Tim recently negotiated the purchase of some land from a small developer who was trying to run the whole project himself, without bothering to appoint a manager. When Tim met with him, the developer kept delaying while secretly attempting to find another buyer to compete against Tim and thereby persuade Tim to up his offer. In the end, Tim got so tired of the developer's behaviour and delaying tactics that he walked away from the deal. As a result, the developer lost the opportunity to make a great deal of money because he was fixated on how much more he could squeeze from the project. He was only interested in the deal that would earn him the most money, without thought of the outcome for Tim.

The best kind of business is the kind that benefits both parties. Let's look at the winning options.

You win

A great opportunity has presented itself to you. Perhaps you are buying some stock that you can sell at a good profit. By obtaining the units at a low price you know that you have forced the supplier to do the deal at little or no profit to himself. You even suggest to him that if he does this deal then you will do a few more in the future on better terms for him. Yet you know you have no intention of ever buying from him again.

Provided that both the service and product or offering are good, then you are the only winner in this deal. From now on, the supplier has every right to be dubious about you and any subsequent dealings with you. How do you feel about participating in such devious transactions? People treated in this way won't come back for more. You will need to search constantly for new suppliers, which is not the best use of your time. How long will it take before word gets out in your industry of the way you operate?

You have won in the short term, but just as surely have lost in the long term.

They win

Let's look at it from the other side of the fence. You have a great product that a client wants from you. You agree to a sale. Your whole team pulls together to produce the goods in the right format, right colour, right specification. You pull out all the stops to fulfil the order. Then the client says that they cannot possibly pay that price, or that you have to pick up the delivery charges. Your profit margin gets squeezed until it can hardly breathe.

How does it feel when they win and you lose? Are you likely to do business with them again? What would you say if another business asks you about them as a potential purchaser?

What is the difference between this scenario and the previous one? Apart from the fact that you are now the one on the receiving end of poor business ethics or behaviour, there is no difference. It is just another side of the same coin.

You both win

For a sustainable future as a business, you have to seek to develop sustainable win–win relationships, and not just with the suppliers who serve you, but with the clients you serve in turn. By understanding the needs of these two groups and those of your own staff, you can blend the whole to achieve the right mix that enables all parties to feel satisfied and fairly treated.

But what happens when you realize that your company is not the ideal one to provide the services or products that your client needs? What should you do?

You can still create a win–win situation out of this. You probably have a database of people who have the skills or resources that your client needs, so be honest and refer them to a more suitable source. You will probably lose the order, but you will gain hugely in terms of goodwill. Your client will return in the future when he needs one of your products and will spread the word that you are ethical in your business dealings.

Implementing the strategy

You have established your strategy, so planning how you will implement it is the next step. This is very much down to each individual business owner and your own specific goals and circumstances, but here are a few more points to consider before you start to tackle the detail.

- Allocate a set amount of time to be devoted towards implementing your strategy. This could be an hour a day or a half-day session each week, according to your circumstances.

- Draw up a list of the tasks relating to your strategy and prioritize them. Schedule them into your diary or personal organizer.

- Set both medium- and long-term goals in order to give yourself measurable benchmarks along the way. These should include goals for a return on your investment, better use of assets, quicker responses to marketing campaigns and higher yields from sources of referral. You should also create and monitor cash flow and expense forecasts, regularly checking your actual achievements against the forecast numbers.

- Be clear on the human resources you need. Think about the positions you need to fill in order to implement your strategy and the skills required. Recruit accordingly, and don't be shy to seek a second opinion. As an entrepreneur, I recognize the tendency to underestimate the work that needs to be done and in the past I have recruited the wrong people through not taking the time to assess the tasks thoroughly.

- Allocate your resources to the areas of the business where you will see the greatest or the most rapid return. But at the same time, be aware that you will need also to invest in areas such as supply and customer service. Even if away from the public eye, your business needs strong systems and support mechanisms in place.

- As your business grows and moves up a gear, you will have to step away from always working 'in the business' and begin the more important process of working 'on the business'. This should become your chief priority as you begin to work towards greater profit and as you progress through this book.

CHAPTER THREE

Money and finance

Finding the flow

Whatever the size of your business your primary goal has to be to create the optimum financial results – for your business and for yourself. In other words you are in your business to actively count the money! If you can't do this because there is no money to count, then you don't have a business. Frightening but true.

The need to focus on managing money may be obvious for you as the leader and driver of the business, but even if this is the case – are you sure you are making it the priority it needs to be? Beyond you, it is essential that every member of your team understands this vital principle and it's down to you to ensure that they grasp the essence of getting money in quickly, and holding on to it for as long as possible.

We know that business is about money and yet, as small businesses, it is very obvious that the odds are somewhat stacked against us in the financial arena. Approaching the marketplace for funding, the owner of the small business will very likely encounter difficulties.

- The banks may see the small business as more risky and set a higher interest rate on lending than they would to a national or international business.
- There is more likelihood of unpaid debts that could cause the business trouble.

- The small size of the venture means there is little strength in the purchasing arm of the business, so there is little scope for significant discounts from suppliers, particularly in the earliest days and years of the business, when arguably such discounts would be most important.
- The bank overdraft facility is the commonly used way of funding the small business and yet the bank can pull this overnight.
- Increasing paper mountains and legislative burden imposed by banks and regulatory bodies, with financial penalties and fines for non-compliance.

Faced with such an atmosphere of financial constraints and requirements it is vital that the money within your business is managed proactively by yourself and senior colleagues, ensuring the longevity of the business. While you may have a finance person within the business, don't feel that you should leave all matters financial to that person. Instead, be willing to get involved in the subject and understand the impact of management decisions on your finance, and of finance upon your ability to make decisions about the running and operation of your business.

Finding the funding

In Chapter 2 we looked at the importance of leading your business towards the goals you identified through to strategy and planning behaviour. Having decided on the business development and growth route you want, you should now develop your financial strategy, essentially bringing into play the monies and revenues necessary for the business to follow its business plan successfully.

There are different methods of finding funding and how you choose to use and prioritize them will be an individual choice. The following are some of the more commonly used:

- **Bank overdrafts** are perhaps the starting point for business funding, and yet possibly the least secure given that the bank can withdraw the overdraft at short notice if it perceives there to be a risk to its money.
- **Equity funding** is a route to get money into the business and one commonly used by larger businesses and those who have listings on either

the stock market or the Alternative Investment Market (AIM). Investors subscribe to a share issue and receive stock in the company in exchange for their investment. Indeed, the owner may use a share issue to raise cash by selling some of their own shares in the company once the business is seen to be strong. Such a sale of shares can also be the financial reward at exit from the company for the owner who has developed a strong business and installed a good management team.

- **Factoring and invoice discounting** is another route to be considered. In this process you give control of your debt-collection activities to a third party who collects the monies and keeps a percentage of the money collected for itself as its fee. The fact that you get quick payment of your debts (usually within days of the invoice being raised) makes it very attractive, even though the cost of doing so can be more expensive than traditional borrowing.

- **Retaining profits** within the business is a very strong and positive way to strengthen the business finances. By keeping the profits within the business the venture has the benefit of positive cash on deposit or held as reserves to support future growth. The build-up of retained profits sends a clear message to the outside world that shareholders and management have decided to allow this potential dividend to stay with the business. Ironically, the business that holds a lot of cash in this way can find it easier to borrow money at good rates in support of business activity.

When considering the options for funding you must take into account the costs of each approach and use the method which brings you the right benefits for your business. Consider the return to you on using a particular method of borrowing relative to its cost. Also, look carefully at any restrictions that are imposed on you by the institution providing the funding. Does the funding you take limit the flexibility of the business to move with the market during the period that the facility is in place?

The money flow

'The true power of investing is a function of recognizing the way that money flows through life.'

The rest of this chapter looks at cash, how you manage it and how you can increase profitability through better financial management. Most people are in business to generate sufficient profit to sustain their business as a venture – and to do so in such a way that they may also derive personal benefit from it by taking out sufficient money to live on, while leaving enough in the business for the business to grow.

We're going to explore the whole basis of money and how it flows into the business and out again, like the tide rolling in and out. I'm going to share with you ways that you can develop and manage your cash flow so that it becomes one of the core strengths of your venture. Too many businesses pursue the closing of each sale or deal to the neglect or even exclusion of the background work that must go into building up the financial resources of the business.

Your biggest priority is to bring in more money than you spend on operating costs. Once you achieve this, your next job is to increase the gap between what comes in and what goes out. Easier said than done perhaps. But very achievable with the right approach.

'I will not run out of cash' should be the mantra for all small-business owners. When building your business, there may be times when you wonder where the next pound is coming from. Every supplier is desperate for immediate payment, while every customer has a hundred reasons for not settling your bills just yet.

Even if your business is sound and your clients are faithful, mistakes with managing money can still be made and the results are likely to be expensive. Although it might be easy with hindsight to see where you went wrong, it is very tough living with these mistakes – on tenterhooks daily, waiting to see whether your cheques will bounce.

Create a cash-positive business environment

Ensuring your business enjoys positive cash flow through its accounts is a blend of behaviours. You need to collect money in and at the same time allow it to flow out, but at a slower rate and in a lesser proportion to the monies coming in. In order to create an environment where your business enjoys positive and plentiful cash you will need to master the following techniques.

Collecting the debts

Don't stint on this process even though it can seem like you now have to be tough after you were using all your interpersonal skills and charm to get the original sale. Understand that if you are slower at collecting money in than you are at paying your creditors (the people that you owe money to) then you will soon have no money and will quickly be out of business. Too many of the companies that collapse have full order books and not enough real cash in the bank account.

If you are not the person to collect the cash then use someone who can be tenacious and who accepts no excuses from your debtors. Getting your solicitor to send a letter to a stalling debtor can be a relatively inexpensive way of creating some positive movement.

For large amounts of money you should consider the merits of using a factoring or invoice discounting service. The money owed is assigned to be collected by a third-party agency that guarantees to pay you a certain amount of the money owed and to do so by a set time. This can give strength to your ability to forecast the monies due. Such a service, though, would be appointed by yourself at the start of the transaction and therefore long before the debt becomes overdue.

Forecast your cash daily

I know you don't carry a crystal ball to predict what will happen exactly in your business, but the daily forecast comes close. This needs to be done over a consistent period of time and I would suggest this means you forecast for the next twelve weeks. Regardless of what you sell or supply, look at the period of time going forward and start to assess when you think certain funds will come into the business. Are you expecting regular weekly amounts from a steady weekend market trade that is predictable, or are things for you affected by the weather and the seasons? Do your customers buy a few times a year and in large values per purchase, or is it little and often that they spend with you? These trends and your knowledge of them allow you to forecast with a degree of accuracy what your cash flows can be.

Knowing your cash-flow forecast allows you to know what you will have at the bank, as well as what you may need to borrow from the bank, but gives you this awareness weeks or even months before you need it. With this advance information you can plan better, and also be seen to be in a stronger position at the bank by asking for a facility before you need to use it.

Control and reduce your overheads

The small monies add up over time. Try this as an example. If you have twenty staff in your business and each has a printer by their PC, are you getting best value on the print cartridges or ink supplies? If each cartridge were to cost your business £30 and you get through one per employee per month, then you have a cost each month of £600 on ink! That's over £7,000 per year. What if you could get a better deal by buying direct or having the supplies shipped in by mail order? Could you save £2,000 to be spent on something that gets you a better return, or simply save the £2,000 as retained profits? It is easier and cheaper to save a pound than it is to go out and earn the same amount.

The same thinking can apply to any regular overhead costs you have. Sit down with your team and look at the many different items you buy in. Discuss other potential suppliers where you can get a better deal. Ask if all the costs need to be as high as they are.

Maintain the lowest stock levels

Forecasting your sales and therefore your cash position gives you an understanding of your stock levels. Stock sitting idle on the shelf does not bring cash into the business or make you a profit, and so you should take care to manage your stock carefully. When you have poor cash flow you should monitor stock levels to make sure that stock is not tying up funds unnecessarily. The time to buy stock in is when you have strong cash flow, not least because then you have the power to negotiate price discounts.

Maintain the maximum financing available

When your business is strong and the cash is coming in, it is so tempting to think it will always be like this that you forget to plan for the slow times or for the downturns in your industry sector. Using your forecasting behaviour and showing your cash reserves, always negotiate a higher overdraft facility with your bank than you think you will need. Lenders get more upset if you exceed your agreed overdraft limit than if you are a little late in making loan repayments. Overdraft abuse screams in the ears of the banker. Set this borrowing limit when you don't need it at the time and you will score more brownie points than if you demand it when the business is against the wall.

Lease, don't buy

As your venture expands and grows there will be a temptation to buy assets such as cars, machinery and equipment. This can tie up cash that could be used more profitably in the business, and in such circumstances it might make better financial sense for you to lease the items. You put down a small deposit, claiming back the interest costs on servicing the debt, and keep more of your own cash in the business.

Build and maintain a strong balance sheet

As you grow you will inevitably need to involve lenders and institutions in supporting you through borrowings. They will take comfort from the strength of your balance sheet and the assets portrayed through this. Likewise, as you seek to open supplier accounts, they will want to see your balance sheet before they commit to extending credit to you.

Make your balance sheet a useful tool in helping you to raise finance and credit. Your accountant will be able to help you structure your balance sheet so that it reflects the business in the best possible way to potential lenders and suppliers, giving them confidence in your ability to pay as the bills fall due.

The profit and loss account is a good way to start with determining how you wish your results to be seen and interpreted. You can show the growth of profits or reduce these to minimize the tax burden in a subsequent year. Before deciding which direction you take the profit and loss account in, you would need to consider the impact on your business, and how you would then make use of the accounts once they have been filed. In such matters always take professional advice from a qualified professional, working with them to achieve the best outcome for your business.

Tracking the movement of cash through your business

As we have already discussed in Chapter 2, having a well-thought-out strategy is vital to the successful running of your business, but putting your strategy into effect requires a healthy cash flow. Cash flows into and out of the business in cycles. Think about your business and analyze how the cash moves within it and through it. When does it come in and from where? When does it need to go out again? Ask yourself the following kinds of questions to spot patterns and trends:

- How often do you invoice – once a week, once a month?
- How many invoices do you raise on each occasion?
- Do you sell a few high-value items a year, or many low-value items more frequently, or something else?
- Do you sell for cash or do you offer credit?
- If credit, what are the terms?
- Do you supply the retail market or a business-to-business audience at wholesale?
- Do you sell via the Internet, via mail order or from a shop?
- Do you broker sales for other people and other businesses?

By thinking about your answers to these questions you will gain a better understanding of your business.

If we take the first question, 'How often do you invoice?', this can be interpreted several ways. If you supply a client with goods four times a month, and only invoice for the total amount at the end of the month, then the client is in effect getting eight weeks to pay for the first order you shipped, seven for the second, and so on, assuming you ask for 28-day payment. If you invoiced with each shipment also asking for 28-day payment, then assuming the client pays on time, you will be improving your cash flow.

Looking at question three, 'Do you sell a few high-value items a year, or many low-value items more frequently, or something else?', we can again extract great value by interpreting your answer.

If you supply four items a year at £75,000 each, your sales turnover is 4 × £75,000, or £300,000 a year. Assuming these sales are made once every three months then you would need to ask yourself if the three months between sales is covered adequately by the revenues received from the prompt payment of the previous invoice. If it was not paid on time, did this cause your business to struggle? Would you do better to request partial payment in advance, maybe 30% or 50% of the order, with the result that you wait shorter periods of time between each payment to the business.

Question four asks, 'Do you sell for cash or do you offer credit?' This could mean asking yourself if everything you supply is paid for in full on the day of delivery, or if you allow people a few days or weeks to settle their bill. If they are not paying on delivery or supply, then you need to understand that you are giving them credit and you must work out whether you can afford this and whether you wish to continue allowing this.

On very expensive items you might approach a finance house for loans that you can offer, in effect connecting your customer with the finance company, in much the same way as happens with furniture, high-value audio equipment, cars and even holidays.

Alternatively, you may decide that what you offer is the sort of item that a client would put on their credit card. In this case you will need to approach your bank for a credit-card package, often referred to as merchant service facilities. The bank will set these up for you and allow you to begin taking credit-card payment from your clients. In this way you are in effect introducing credit rather than giving it yourself. The client applies to put the purchase price on their credit card and you get the funds within a few days direct to your business account, minus the inevitable percentage charge levied by the credit-card company.

Many businesses find that accepting credit-card payment allows them to sell far more than when they accepted only cash or cheques. Try this for yourself.

Analyze the answers to all the other questions in the same way as we have done here. The questions here and elsewhere are prompts for more thinking, provoking you into analyzing and assessing your business. In the course of the book we raise many questions. They are designed to ask you about your business so that you think more about the processes that you go through. By being aware of the things you are doing, some unintentionally, you will be better placed to make and implement positive change through new behaviours.

Take time to look at why your answers are what they are, and determine if they could have a different outcome. However, to expect to get a different outcome from your business when you are still applying the behaviour that has got you to where you are now, would be ludicrous. You need to change the stimulus if you are to get a different response.

You do not have to change anything that is working, unless you feel that you could take the ideas supplied here and make things work even better. Often just one small idea can have a hugely positive impact when applied correctly, but that does require that you fully understand how your business works in the first place.

Regular income, growing business

When you start out, your survival as a fledgling business depends upon the regular nature of your income, almost regardless of the amount. This is because even when income is low, it is possible to find a bank that will lend to you, providing money is flowing in regularly. As the business grows and the incoming amounts become larger, your position grows in line with the deposits you hold at the bank. When the business becomes more mature, you can generate investment income from the money you accumulate and enjoy a strong sense of independence from the marketplace.

Growing profit is an important way of taking the business forward and one that is also an easy way of measuring your progress. There are many aspects of your business that can be analyzed and there are many books about management ratios, formulas, statistics, etc. I am not attempting to compete with these. Instead, I want you to look at your business in a different way and focus on the cash flow itself, rather than the way it has been generated.

In our *Small Business, Big Profit!* seminars we often meet business owners with ten, twenty, perhaps fifty staff, but who still don't allocate sufficient time to understanding and analyzing their figures. It need not be the frightening process you might think. In fact, acknowledging what you might have missed by not carrying out this type of analysis is likely to be far more scary. Spending some quality time with your calculator analyzing your figures will teach you a great deal and will far outweigh the effort required in making the study.

Key figures

Here are a few examples of the kinds of questions that you should be asking about your *Small Business, Big Profit!* business.

- What are your sales per employee? (Simply divide your sales turnover by the number of staff you have.)

- How does this figure compare with those of your competitors in the industry?

- What are your gross (total) and net (less salary, car, bonuses, etc.) sales per salesperson?

- What is the average monetary sum invoiced for your client sales? In different divisions?

- What is the 'lifetime value' of a customer to your business? This is the total amount of money you receive from a client during the entire time that they do business with you.

- What return do you get per thousand pounds or euros of advertising? Break this down into the revenue derived from classified adverts, display adverts, magazine or newsletter, banner adverts on the Internet, links with other websites, by national or regional segment, etc.

- What is your gross and net profit margin per transaction? Break it down and calculate it for different product ranges, activities and markets, etc.

- What is the percentage spread of revenue from the different areas of your business? For example, how much revenue is generated from advertising, from attending business clubs, professional networking events and trade and industry exhibitions, from media and PR leads, old-fashioned word of mouth, existing client referral, direct response marketing, cold calls, local account management, and so on? Working out which aspects and areas of your business generate the most income helps you direct the focus of your time and energies.

- What is the financial value of repeat business? This is business from your existing clients who are already on your database and are buying from you, whether you prompt them or not. Are you scoring the sales figures when you do prompt them and noting which ways of prompting are achieving the best results?

Understanding your bank

Both small and big businesses love to bitch about banks. They'll lend you an umbrella when it's not raining and seize it back when the heavens open, as the story goes. This is really a 'dig' at money lending in general. But, whatever you think of them, as the owner of a *Small Business, Big Profit!* venture, you need to *understand* how banks 'think'.

I worked for five years in the international arm of a major bank. It was exciting, interesting and sometimes even glamorous to work on the 34th floor of a skyscraper in the heart of London. Yet the hardest work I ever did there was during a month's assignment to the bank's small-business team. I had to observe the flow of receipts in and loans out to the customers and sat in on dozens of meetings with small-business owners and lending officers. This was an education in itself and has proved to be of great value to me!

Typically, business owners would call in without an appointment or arrange one at just a few days notice, wanting to borrow money temporarily on an overdraft or in the form of a long-term loan. What amazed me was the consistently limited amount of information the client would provide and yet still expect the bank to hand over the money.

From years of running my own business I know that it is not always possible to predict what businesses need in terms of short-term financing.

However, it was quite an eye-opener to see engineers present their requirements on a scrap of paper, or IT consultants to hand over a two-thousand word document written in technospeak. If you want your bank to be there for you when you need it most, the secret is regular communication. It's as simple as that.

I know we are talking about your business and that the account handler probably looks like a teenager fresh from school, but while this may be irksome, it is irrelevant: you need to make a friend of your bank. The bottom line is that you will need to borrow money at some time or other, and probably more frequently than you would like. In the early days you borrow to stay afloat, launch a new product line, fund some research . . . Later, you may need funding to purchase some machinery, new computer equipment, to develop a property or to enhance your product development.

It is your job to persuade the bank that you are a good bet. How do you go about this?

- Check your account balance every day.
- Be aware of what money is going out each day.
- Monitor expected revenue each week and look ahead several weeks, to know what money you can expect to come in.
- Send your bank your business plan.
- Talk it through with your account manager.
- At least once a month, telephone the bank and speak with your contact there.
- Once a month, send them your forecast for the next three months.
- Have on hand comparisons of previous months' cash flow so that the bank can compare like with like.
- Advise them about business that you are chasing or are likely to win.
- Above all – keep them involved and keep them informed.

Put yourself in your bank manager's shoes. He receives a call from a business owner who has had little contact with his branch to date. Nevertheless, the owner is seeking to borrow money at short notice, but has supplied the bank manager with scant information about the core aspects of his business. In such a position, is the bank manager likely to regard the request very favourably? Get real.

Ten key questions to ask yourself about your cash and your bank

1 Is your money working for you?

2 What can you do to strengthen your finances?
New products
More promotion and marketing
Increased pricing
Greater sales figures
More frequent sales
Acquiring new clients

3 Where is your business plan? How recent is it?

4 Why have you not written one / updated it recently?

5 When did you last explain your business to your bank?

6 How do you manage and monitor the financial transactions in your business?

7 How do you interpret the information for greater profit?

8 How often do you get referral contacts from your bank?

9 If you needed to borrow money at short notice, are you confident your bank would help you?

10 How rigorously do you chase up unpaid invoices?

If you don't know the answers to more than half the above questions or can't answer them positively, then you have a lot of work to do. Regular and positive cash flow is absolutely fundamental to keeping your business running, while a detailed analysis of that cash flow is vital to assess its profitability.

Financial strategies and money mentalities

Think back to the reasons you wanted to create your *Small Business, Big Profit!* venture in the first place. Look back at Chapter 1 and remember the motivators that caused you to kick the whole thing off. How many of these were financially driven? Can you remember what they were? Try to be specific. Remind yourself also of your business strategy from Chapter 2. Different strategies require different responses in terms of money. To stay small but become more profitable is one route, but totally distinct from staying small and not seeking anything more than just keeping your head above water. Unfortunately, many businesses get stuck in this position without any idea of how to get out of it.

When is a business really a job?

Let's look at different types of business owner and the way they approach their finances.

The first group of people run their businesses with what can only be referred to as a Job Mentality. They may not work for someone else in the eyes of the tax man, but a quick analysis of their thinking reveals that they don't really work for themselves either . . . well, only just. Arriving for work at the shop or office, day in, day out, their income is determined by what other companies will pay them. Hopefully it is sufficient to support the family, pay the bills and perhaps have enough left over to take an annual holiday. But this group places little value on their ability to lead a market trend, to increase their pricing or to devise a new business model for their venture. They have simply swapped their previous experience of being a wage slave for being the owner of a *Small Business, No Profit* venture! Not quite what you had in mind for your own business?

The scary fact is that this group comprises a vast proportion of all small-business owners. If they work hard and acquire a good reputation for customer service, delivery punctuality, etc., they might rise through the ranks of similar ventures to attain a leading position. But there is a passive expectancy to simply maintain the business and bring home a regular salary each month. Cutting their cloth according to the revenue received from the business, by accepting less income, they are also creating less opportunity for their venture. The truth is that this group have jobs that are masquerading as businesses, rather than healthy, profit-making concerns.

If we look at the money that is earned in such a scenario, it flows like this.

How money works with a Job Mentality

In this scenario, life truly is a struggle. With each cost of living increase or rise in inflation, another pinch is felt in the budget. As new expenditure hits one area, a tightening of the belt has to be made in another. Money flow with a Job Mentality is illustrated in Figure 3.1.

Business owners with this kind of outlook should resign themselves to starting each month in the same position as they were in the previous month. Looking ahead several months or a year can be very demoralizing as there seems little likelihood of any interesting or exciting opportunities appearing on the horizon, and no clear way to progress, or worse, no way out at all. This gloomy world seems to revolve around debt and liabilities.

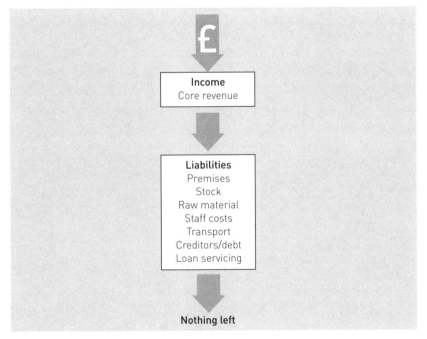

Figure 3.1   Money flow with a Job Mentality

How money works with a Saving Mentality

The second group is more productive and yields a small profit each month. This surplus is set aside as savings or money on deposit. I call this the *Small Business, Small Savings* group; its money flow is illustrated in Figure 3.2.

In this type of operation the money coming in is being used as widely as possible. It takes care of operating expenses, with a small amount being placed in a savings programme each month while still paying off outstanding debts and loans regularly. The crucial factor here is that a feeling of optimism is created by knowing that not all the income is being absorbed by the daily grind, but that some of it is being saved for the future. Rather than being stuck in the daily 9-to-5 rut alternating between home and work, there is a hint of possibility in the air, the sense that the future may hold something more exciting.

It is true that these small-business owners are still running their companies like job replacement activities rather than fully functioning businesses with broader benefits, but the underlying feeling of optimism becomes self-fulfilling. The more hopeful you feel about the future, the more energy you

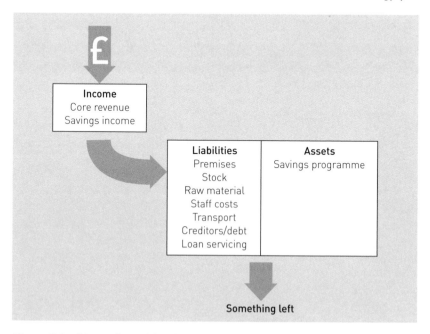

Figure 3.2 Money flow with a Saving Mentality

have and the easier it becomes to work out how to manage your limited resources better. You can visualize things getting better for you. The majority of revenue may still be absorbed into a large and rather frightening black hole named Liabilities, but you are still able to put a small amount of money aside. Provided you put the money to positive use, you have the potential to move forward.

How money works with an Investing Mentality

The regular savings plan has now accumulated sufficient capital for an investment which can itself produce a return in the form of a dividend, or a regular income stream. With steady reinvestment, and bolstered by ongoing savings from job income, the returns on investments increase (see Figure 3.3).

Having created income from several sources, this business owner will be able to acquire more assets from the money that comes from the original asset first acquired.

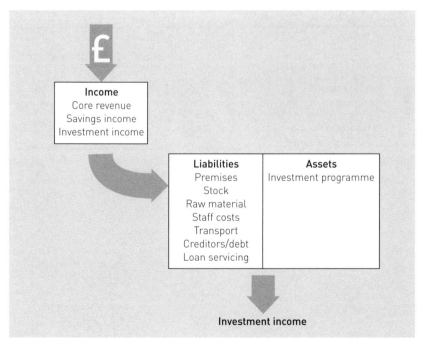

Figure 3.3 Money flow with an Investing Mentality

How money works with a Long-term Investing Mentality

The regular savings have now accumulated sufficiently to create an investment which produces a return in the form of a dividend, a rent roll or a regular income stream. The results of the investment activity are now throwing off regular income that is in a position to grow. As you continue with long-term saving and investing activities, the rate at which your business can buy more performing assets speeds up as more income streams are created. This money flow is illustrated in Figure 3.4.

The investment could be in the form of equities, property or the acquisition of other businesses that have a natural synergy with the original venture. A publishing business that owns both a web design outfit and a small print business would be one such example, or a business that provides frequent training services, and opts to buy a small conference facility rather than spend money on hiring hotel meeting rooms.

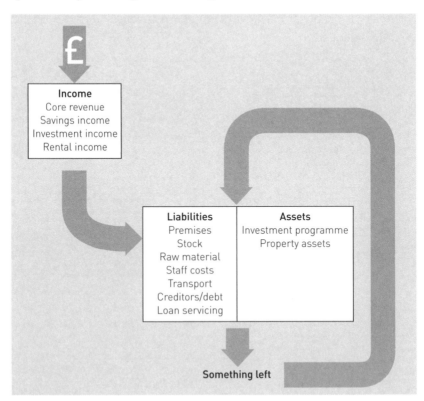

Figure 3.4 Money flow with Long-term Investing Mentality

Having created income from several sources, this business owner will also be able to acquire more assets with the money coming in from the first asset (investment) that was bought.

How money works with a Business Ownership Mentality

Notice how different this cash flow, illustrated in Figure 3.5, is from the first one we looked at. Now the core revenue has all but disappeared because the old business has changed so much. Business ownership dividends and continued investment income are now pumping the cash flow. By reaching this stage you create the structure and the investment vehicle to provide you with an ongoing cash flow for as long as you require.

The new skills and experience you have acquired as you built up the other sub-units or teams increases your knowledge of business ownership, company law and taxation – all areas of knowledge which will benefit you greatly.

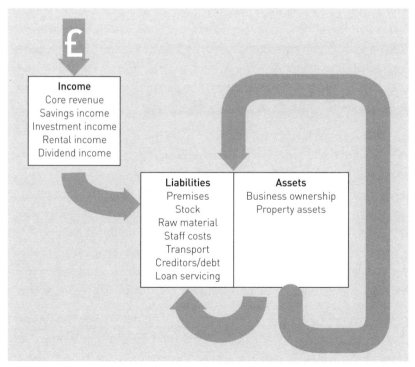

Figure 3.5 Money flow with a Business Ownership Mentality

Developing your investment mentality

The idea that your thoughts create your reality has been around a long time. In the flow charts we looked at how different kinds of mental outlook and behaviour in relation to money determine what part income plays in your business. We have seen how easily you can make money work for you to improve your circumstances and create further income streams.

However, it takes discipline to become a successful saver, and to progress from simple saving to becoming a successful investor. The amounts of money might, and hopefully will, get larger, but the principles of investing remain the same.

Spending money on the usual business consumables such as printing, paper, pens, advertising, memberships, etc., yields no obvious or long-lasting return. It is all too easy to waste funds by buying more stationery than you need, paying for taxis rather than incurring a vehicle financing bill, attending seminars and then not distributing your handouts to colleagues. Money spent on a paperback novel can give you a feel-good factor for a few hours, but the same funds spent on a business how-to book can stimulate ideas and different ways of looking at your own business. Once you have implemented any suitable ideas, pass the book on to others in your team for their input. Even just one useful idea from such a book could create a measurable payback for the business for years to come.

The essence of an investment mentality is not to squander money but to put it to good use, and ensure that it replaces itself continually. But the investment need not always be in conventional assets. Money can be put to equally good use in other, more imaginative ways. What about enrolling in an evening class? Furthering your knowledge or learning new skills in existing areas will impact directly upon your performance in the workplace. As a result, more revenue flows in, which you can reinvest in more training. And don't dismiss the intangible benefits of all this. Your increased expertise makes you stronger and more positive mentally as well as financially.

Equally, acquiring an investment mentality should make you use business revenue more prudently. It will make you think twice about buying a new car on borrowed funds until the debt on the previous one has been paid off.

You might be able to identify ways of using the car to pay for itself, or decide to claim tax relief on car expenses and costs when previously you might not have bothered.

The key to begin developing strong income from business assets lies in how you use the money that is available to you now. The point is not really how much or how little you have as surplus each month, but rather that you start to utilize the power of compound interest and put it to work for your company's benefit.

I recently read an article in the business pages of a respected national news-paper. The headline was 'Small Businesses to Shut Their Doors' and was about owners deciding to shut down rather than keep on making losses. Yet, the angle missed by the journalist was that the businesses featured were doomed to make losses if they refused to embrace new technology, step beyond their sales comfort zones and enter new markets, or to adapt to changing consumer requirements. Instead of looking at ways to improve their financial situation, these business owners were closing down and seeking the 'safety' offered by a regular 9-to-5 job!

Developing your approach to the duplication of time and skill

Here the focus is on the creation of a business that will give you the oppor-tunity to duplicate your time, and the scope to create ongoing income streams.

Most businesses never manage the first step of duplicating themselves. Obvious exceptions are many of the world's most successful franchise brands. The franchisee buys into a system of teaching and training that has been developed previously by the franchisor. The quick access to this accu-mulated knowledge is what gives the new franchise owner the opportunity to learn from the mistakes that have already been made. This leaves them free to concentrate on the purpose of the business – making money and profit.

Whether your goal is to operate your venture from one location or three, it is crucial you understand what the money does, how it works, and how much the income from each operation affects your current earnings and gives you fresh options.

Take a look at the following examples. All these businesses are small, but the difference in turnover is striking.

Example 1

Michael	Engineering consultancy	
	1 part-time administrator	
	Turnover €120,000	
Core revenue	Consulting	€ 98,000
	(Engineering in manufacturing processes)	
Poorly defined	Occasional speaking at events	€ 7,000
Secondary		
revenues	Introduction fees from product suppliers	€ 15,000
		€120,000

Michael works alone as a jobbing consultant, finding work when he can, not daring to charge too much for fear of losing out to his competitors. He has a part-time administrator helping him with paperwork, but she is largely underutilized.

Example 2

Adriana	Web design and Internet solutions	
	3 employees	
	Turnover £350,000	
Core revenue	Web design	£180,000
Second income	Shopping cart customization	£ 80,000
Third income	Tailoring presentation graphics for conferences	£ 65,000
Other Incomes	Consultancy for local businesses	£ 25,000
		£350,000

This is a small business that has developed reasonably strong revenues in a number of areas. With minimal effort other than focusing on what it does well, it is reasonable to suppose that this business could expand by 10% a year. How? Just take each of the four current revenue streams and look to increase them by 10%, i.e. web design an extra £18,000, shopping carts £8,000, graphics £6,500 and local consultancy £2,500.

Hardly rocket science, but designed to be simple to make the point!

Example 3

Jack and Beth	Rocking horse manufacturers 2 employees Turnover C$516,000	
Core revenue	Hand-carved rocking horses	C$280,000
Second income	Carved household furniture	C$130,000
Third income	Books on carving and woodcrafts	C$ 56,000
Fourth income	Regular auctions of children's toys	C$ 50,000
		C$516,000

This crafts and carpentry business, based in a semi-rural location, trades more than half a million Canadian dollars in the niche market of rocking horses. The horses produced are exquisite and sell for as much as C$20,000 per item, with clients spending extra dollars on accessories. Many are bought by collectors.

Realizing they could produce more with their workspace, Jack and Beth employed two staff so that the company could produce additional products from the same raw materials. The secondary income they receive from these products now comprises more than 20% of their income, but utilizes the same production resources. Often, a sale of furniture leads to a more specialized purchase and, in response to client requests, they have tailored other areas of the business to suit their market, developing these as sources of income. The business owners in this example have the highest turnover of the three and also make and retain the strongest profits through dividends to themselves.

Hanging on to the money

Contrary to what you might learn from the media, most business owners don't drive Bentleys, sport diamond-encrusted Rolex watches or buy small islands in the Pacific. Well, some might to make a statement, but in terms of managing money the majority of the more successful business owners only take from their business what the business can comfortably afford. The less you withdraw from the business in salaries and dividends the more there is to be reinvested, either in commercial markets for investment, or back into the business and its enhanced performance.

Retaining money in the business is best illustrated by the use of balance sheets and asset statements. These give you a snapshot of the business at a given moment in time, usually at the end of each accounting period.

The core of the balance sheet looks like this:

Balance sheet

Assets	Liabilities
Cash deposits	Business loans
Property	Rent agreements
Machinery	Vehicle finance
Debtors	Loans

Clearly the value of the left-hand 'asset' column should be greater than the right-hand 'Liabilities' column. The right-hand column shows what you owe – to other businesses, to the bank, to individuals who helped you get started, etc.

Your assets should cover your liabilities many times over. For example, if your cash deposits (an asset) represent the same amount as your loans (a liability), but are less than the total amount of liabilities, *potentially* you are in a difficult situation.

Where the assets total three or four times your liabilities, clearly you have built up some breathing space.

An ideal place in which to be and one which places you in a position of power, is where your income from just some of your revenue-producing assets is equal to or greater than your business operating expenses.

To illustrate this, let's look at how two businesses treat the renting out of workspace:

1 Stephen has a duplex office unit on a small town business park. He purchased this for £100,000 and he receives an income in rent from the business downstairs of £8,000 a year, or 8% of his original gross price investment.

2 On the same business park, David and Samantha have bought three units and rent each one out for £15,000, receiving a total of £45,000 rent against their original gross investment of £300,000 for the units. These units are assets that David and Samantha chose to invest in, seeing the long-term potential for commercial rentals.

Stephen is receiving income that goes some way to offset the loan repayment on his unit. David and Samantha bought their units with cash originally, and their income from the units covers their living expenses, making them financially independent by reason of their rental income – their asset supplies the revenue.

CHAPTER FOUR

Making it run smoothly

Systems and processes

The phone rings, interrupting your train of thought, but it's an important call so you have to take it. The courier in the hallway needs your signature for a package . . . 'just a couple of seconds'! A knock at the door heralds the arrival of someone needing just two minutes of your time . . . which rapidly become twenty. A dozen emails demand action . . . now! A familiar scenario?

Attending to the urgent diverts attention from the important and I'll bet this fractured and frantic routine is all too recognizable. It's probably a far cry from the way you had imagined your working day, dealing with emails before the phone started ringing, sorting out sales enquiries, converting potential clients to paying customers, then clearing your desk and leaving on schedule for a family meal at home. Is that how it was supposed to be?

Along the way the work piled up and perhaps you hired some help but found your staff to be less committed than you, particularly if they didn't have a stake in the venture. Perhaps you have cash flow problems, the spectre that haunts all small businesses. The trouble is, you are too busy fulfilling orders to chase up debts. Or perhaps customers have told you that they had difficulty finding you again after you moved offices and you know you must have lost repeat business as a result.

What can you do to remedy all this and turn your *Small Business* into a well-oiled *Big Profit!* machine?

SSPs to the rescue

You are not a robot, although at times you may feel like one when lack of time for rest and relaxation deprives you of the ability to think straight, let alone think with any spark of creativity or originality. Juggling the demands of your personal and working life is tough enough, but when you have your own business it sometimes seems impossible. How can you retain some semblance of a personal life, make time for your family and yet also make real progress at work?

You don't need to call on the services of a chisel jawed super-hero clad in Lycra, you just need to install some SSPs – Systems, Structures and Processes – that will get the business running smoothly, minimize mistakes and free up some of your time to boot.

Here's why SSPs are so important:

- You learn that it's the service that clients want, not the person who delivers it.
- You learn that others can do a job as well as you, so you can delegate freely.
- Efficient systems also free up your time to concentrate on what you do best.
- Your employees have a chance to take on increased responsibility, and the broadening of their roles leads to increased satisfaction and happier staff.
- More thinking time means you can develop further revenue streams to increase profitability and think strategically, rather than reactively.
- More free time means you have more control over how you use your time and helps you to achieve a better work/life balance.
- Systems lead to increased efficiency, enabling more clients to be served in the same amount of time and therefore profitability to be increased.
- Systems also minimize the opportunities to make mistakes.

- You will be able to create an efficiently run business that will be ripe for selling on, should you wish to do so.

The importance of developing your own SSP technology

By 'SSP technology' I simply mean the systems that are tailored to your company's needs that will enable you to achieve your business goals in the shortest possible time.

The systems you install will depend upon the nature of your business, but there are two key areas that apply to most businesses.

1. Letting go . . . a little

You created your business and you are the person who understands it best, but this does not mean that you are the only person capable of working in it. Handing over some of your tasks to others will free up your time and contribute to increased profitability. Even if reaching the point of employing staff seems a long way off, if you want your venture to succeed, you must learn to let others help you when the time is right.

I have already touched upon the importance of delegation and taking on staff in terms of your strategy, but this really is a key point and I will return to it again. The most important thing to remember when employing staff is that they should either contribute directly to the bottom line, or they should free up someone else to do so.

CASE IN POINT

Marie operates an IT support call-centre with eighteen staff. The three teams of six each have a team leader who is a qualified computer engineer with specialized knowledge. The other members of each team have a good working knowledge of the systems they support, but are not experts in all of them. Marie and her team leaders have the core knowledge, but are only involved in certain of the incoming calls.

Each employee has an on-screen call handler script, suggesting how incoming calls should be handled according to the nature of the enquiry. On the rare occasions that they are unable to resolve the issue, a call-back system is in place.

Although Marie set up the business and has a thorough knowledge of it, she does not handle many of the calls herself. Her chief role is to formulate strategy, refine systems and seek out new business. With areas of expertise that sometimes duplicate but also complement each other, each team leader and five handlers can deal with a wide range of calls. None of the team leaders has knowledge of the business in its entirety yet their areas of expertise dovetail to produce a highly effective workforce.

2. Consistency and reliability

Do you visit the same coffee shop every morning on your way to work? Do you browse in the same bookstore chain whichever town you're in, or stay in the same hotel chain when you travel? You remain a loyal customer because you know exactly what to expect. Companies spend millions on ensuring that you revisit their brand time and again. A core part of their business is ensuring they give you the same experience with each visit. They know that by guaranteeing a certain level of service, you will feel safe using them and are likely to come back again.

Have you ever worked hard to secure a new client and supplied them on several occasions only to have them subsequently disappear? Have you considered why this should be? The most likely reason is that your service was not consistent enough for them to feel confident in continuing with you. They want and expect to have the same level of service each time they do business with you. Your role should be to ensure that, regardless of who within your company is doing the work, the client has the same experience and receives the same level of service every time.

CASE IN POINT

Frank is a one-man car-washing business, operating from a car park on the edge of town. He was not too expensive and did a reasonable job. The first time I used his services, he set to work with buckets, water and a fair dollop of elbow grease and twenty minutes later, the result was a spotless car. I was very pleased.

The second time he left a few soapy smears by not rinsing thoroughly. However, the interior of the car was spick and span and his attitude was good. The third time, he washed the car well, valeted the interior but forgot to empty the ashtrays and didn't clean the interior of the windscreen.

I never went back a fourth time. I could not predict in advance what my experience would be. It was this unpredictability more than anything that prevented me from using Frank again.

The moral of this particular story is that Frank is losing repeat business simply because he is unaware, firstly, that his service is uneven, and secondly, that maintaining a consistent standard is of importance. As a result, he needs to find a constant supply of new clients to maintain his turnover. This does not make good business sense. Servicing the same clients regularly would make better use of his time and allow him to build up his client base further, having a direct and positive impact on his bottom line.

Look at all aspects of your business

Take a close look at your venture to study what systems are already in place and how effective they are. Learn to monitor and measure them. Take a look at those that are less than satisfactory. What is wrong and how could you set about improving them? Make sure that the systems you install to improve them will also alert you to when they fall below par.

The requirements of each company are different, but here are a few general questions to set you thinking:

- What are your strengths as a company? What do you do well?
- Which are the parts that are the most profitable?
- How consistent is the level of your service or the quality of your products?
- How are you providing the current levels of service that you offer?
- What part of your offering could be improved and what simple steps could you take to make the improvement?
- Are there any products or services that you are confident you have delivered well, yet which have not led to repeat orders?
- What systems do you use to keep in touch with people and do you get the best out of them? How do you use email, database software, customer relationship management (CRM) software, voicemail, wireless technology, etc.
- What do you need to do to make it easy for your clients to buy from you again and again? As explained in the previous chapter, repeat business should add handsomely to your bottom line. Remember:
  - If you make it easy for clients to return, they will.
  - If you make it easy for them to refer others to your services, they will.
  - If you provide an opportunity for them to spend money repeatedly, they will.
- How many of the job positions in your business do not contribute to the end product or service?
- Do you have any staff who perform well and are clearly client-centred, but who are not customer facing?

Tailoring systems to your need – the Process Folder

An example of a system that we devised in our own businesses is our Process Folder. This collates all the information that enables each employee to understand what is expected of them and become familiar with those parts of the business that relate to their role specifically. It evolved when we first made the leap from being a two-person home-based business to a business with five employees and needed to pass on the mass of experience we had accumulated as the business founders.

I looked at the franchise system and it was very clear that the most successful operations are the ones with the best training programmes for new staff when the franchise is being set up. I chose not to take the franchising route, but I could see that there would be clear benefits from emulating their systems in our own business.

Knowing that we would not always be on hand in person to explain each role and the systems we had established, we began to write notes. By the time we were recruiting our third and fourth staff members we realized that time was being wasted writing the same note each time a new staff member was hired – hence the notes developed into a folder.

Now each new member of the team is inducted more by their colleagues than by myself and the Process Folder allows them to understand their role in detail, with little being omitted or open to misinterpretation. A copy of the Process Folder now sits by each desk.

Set aside some time to analyze your own business and imagine that you are going to sell part of it as a franchise. What would the prospective franchisees need to know in order to replicate your operation? How would you explain to them about answering the telephone, handling an email enquiry, ordering stationery, winning new business, etc.?

Writing it all down

A mission statement, or a brief explanation of why you started your business and what you set out to achieve, is a good starting point for your own

Process Folder. Telling staff what you did before the business, how it has grown, where client groups come from, and so on, gives new staff an important historical perspective. Follow this with sections on answering the telephone, finding new clients, handling emails, raising an invoice, etc.

Don't be embarrassed to write up a process that is *apparently* as straight-forward as how the telephone should be answered. I promise you that just the simple act of attempting to write this down will force you to make choices about the procedure and how it represents your business.

To help you make a start, here are some areas which could benefit from the introduction of a system or procedure, but obviously there are many more:

- Structuring a job advert
- Managing a recruitment interview
- Introducing the business to prospective clients
- Explaining your vision, to staff or the bank
- Drafting a press release
- Designing promotional business literature
- Hosting a meeting
- Speaking in front of an audience
- Running an exhibition
- Implementing a compensation and benefits policy to reward staff
- Compiling a Process Folder or reviewing an existing handbook
- Handling incoming mail and email
- Dealing with a complaint
- Creating a sales strategy template
- Designing an order form
- Processing a mail order purchase
- Issuing a refund on a purchase
- Structuring a new supplier contract

CASE IN POINT

Mitchell is a grain merchant. He supplies seed, fertilizer and some crop protection products to farmers, large agricultural estates, municipal parkland and some private homes.

For a long time Mitchell's biggest headache was the collection of debts. He has now developed scripts to guide the staff who chase up outstanding debts on the phone. These scripts form part of his Process Folder and cover various stages in the credit control process – alerting a client that the permitted credit period has been exceeded, asking for prompt payment, warning that legal action will be sought if there is no response, and so on.

Mitchell is convinced that the adoption of this simple system has been a major breakthrough. 'Prior to this', he says, 'I was running from task to task, not stopping to think why I was constantly repeating myself and starting each task from scratch all the time. Now I share the work with others rather than think I always know best. Our customers have given us very positive feedback on how the business is now better at serving them consistently.'

Use SSPs creatively

SSPs need not be confined to the traditional areas of your business such as managing mail, handling sales, invoicing, etc. Here are a couple of examples of other areas in which they can be of use.

Duplicating yourself professionally

It is not just your business that will benefit from the consideration and implementation of SSP technologies. What about you? As owner, director and leader of your business, you are almost certainly distracted by matters which, if dealt with effectively, could mean an increase in your own productivity. For example, SSP technology allows you to 'make more of who you are' by helping you to increase your presence in your industry. It does this through simple applications that allow you to 'duplicate' yourself and be in several places at once. Here are a few suggestions:

- Auto responder messages from web adverts (automatically generated response messages)
- Telephone management services, with both operator (such as at a call centre) and voicemail provision
- Paper and e-based newsletters
- CD-based and web-driven audio information files (such as a newsletter)
- Virtual assistants

As well as duplicating yourself, you can duplicate your venture, or parts of it. See Chapter 3 for more on this.

Locking clients into your business

It is less costly in terms of time and money to retain a client who is already purchasing from you than to attract and sign up a new one, but you want to achieve both. Think about what kind of SSP you could install that would lock your clients in automatically, allowing you to keep their custom, providing valuable repeat income with only minimal effort. (See also Chapter 8, page 117–119.)

A good example of this is the loyalty card, where a business such as a fast-food outlet or a dry cleaner hands out a small card containing ten boxes. Every time a client makes a purchase or has an item cleaned, the card is stamped. When the tenth box is stamped, the transaction is free. A simple device, but one that is highly effective.

Don't neglect the 'little touches' in this respect. The small things that you can do to show your appreciation all serve to lock in your clients. As I travel about the country a great deal, I seem to be forever buying fuel for the car. In most cases it is a soulless transaction, but the staff of one fuel station break the mould in a small but significant way and it makes a huge difference in terms of my appreciation. As the cashier hands my credit card back to me he acknowledges my name (having read it from the card) with a simple, 'Thank you, Mr Rampley-Sturgeon'. Although I know the staff are taught this technique and educated in its use by the owner, it still comes across as genuine and unusual client care. It is the implementation of 'little touches' that you can employ to make clients reluctant to switch to a competitor.

Technology

Make the best use of technology to manage information without overload. If you have to wade through scores of emails that are copied 'for information' every morning in order to get to those that will contribute something concrete to the business, your staff are not using the system correctly. Copying the world and his wife in on an email is a security blanket for the sender made easy by the technology. It absolves the sender of responsibility by being able to say they copied the message to X, Y and Z. Ensure staff only copy in those who really need to know about an issue and avoid information overload. Email is a wonderful tool, but it can be abused very easily. In a *Small Business, Big Profit!* venture, responsibility is everything.

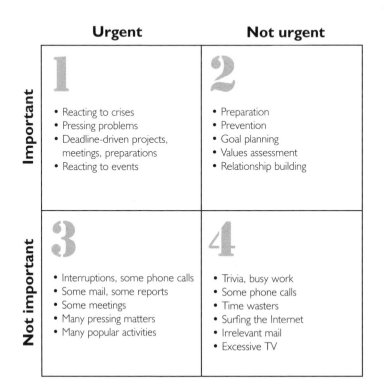

	Urgent	**Not urgent**
Important	1 • Reacting to crises • Pressing problems • Deadline-driven projects, meetings, preparations • Reacting to events	2 • Preparation • Prevention • Goal planning • Values assessment • Relationship building
Not important	3 • Interruptions, some phone calls • Some mail, some reports • Some meetings • Many pressing matters • Many popular activities	4 • Trivia, busy work • Some phone calls • Time wasters • Surfing the Internet • Irrelevant mail • Excessive TV

Similarly, think about your database management systems. Used correctly, these are of enormous benefit, but data should not need to be input more than once, this is a total waste of staff resources. Ensure your system suits your requirements, and that once data have been input, information can be fed into the company's other systems without too much additional work.

Putting SSP technology in place will make your business stronger and pave the way for increased profitability. And as you introduce and implement these systems, you may well discover that you enjoy your business more because of the new-found control and understanding that the systems have given you.

Beware the time stealers

Time stealers are behavioural patterns and issues that can hold you back or that have an extremely damaging, time-wasting effect. Should you own up to any? They can leave you feeling frustrated and unhappy at your lack of control, so take steps to remedy the situation immediately.

Self-inflicted time stealers

- **Negative attitude** – A negative attitude makes it hard to get up in the morning. Resolve to look for five positive things every day. Even if they are as simple as managing to unblock the photocopier quickly, they will be there. Look for them and enjoy them. Be positive.

- **Leisure activities** – It is pretty obvious, but too much time spent in the bar, or checking out the bargains on eBay eats into your working day. You need to relax, and achieving a good work/life balance is vital to your own well-being, but it is equally important to get the mix right.

- **Failing to delegate or to allow others to contribute** – Free up some of your time to concentrate on the things that you do best, such as planning long-term strategy.

- **Indecision** – A simple lack of information can often be the cause of a paralyzing inability to make a decision. Get together all the information you can and DO make that decision. If you don't, someone else might make it for you and not necessarily in your favour. And even wrong decisions can have a positive aspect as you can learn from your mistakes.

- **Fear of the unknown** – 'What if' scenarios can be seriously discouraging. Research the situation, check out your options, get the information you need. Once the unknown is known, it loses its power to intimidate.

- **Procrastination** – What are you afraid of accomplishing? Once you have taken the first steps towards tackling a task, you will feel a whole lot better and your achievements will gather momentum as the day progresses.

- **Fear of change** – It is all too easy to stick with what you know. Change involves the unknown. Conquer your fear by focusing on the fact that you will succeed, and not only that, you will also enjoy it. Be brave enough to welcome innovation. If you were bold enough to start your business in the first place, there is no need to fear any of the changes that might be required along the way.

- **Lack of self-discipline** – If you can accomplish the goals you set yourself for each day, you will feel a great sense of achievement, leading to increased happiness and self-esteem. If you make a habit of long lunches and getting in late, you will fritter away your time in an unproductive manner.

- **Being disorganized** – a major time waster and detrimental to the smooth running of the company. Make sure you are sufficiently organized to follow your daily plan and accomplish the tasks you set yourself. Keep your work area tidy and free from any papers except those on which you are working. You need to be able to access information, files and notes quickly and without stress. Avoid handling paper more than a couple of times without actioning it.

- **Lack of vision and clear goals** – Everything we do well is based on a clear goal. A hazy or an ill-defined goal is really nothing more than a vague wish. A vision drives you forward. If you don't have a goal, how can you move on?

- **Tiredness and fatigue** – Your physical well-being is your responsibility. Regular exercise, a good balanced diet and sufficient sleep are the essential ingredients to keep you feeling well and mentally alert. Your contribution to the company is vital, so look after yourself.

- **Lack of a clear direction in the workforce** – The cost to the bottom line of a confused workforce can be enormous, and lack of direction leads to dissatisfaction and low morale. Make sure your staff understand what they are doing and why.

- **Overcommitment** – It is difficult to say no to the offer of work, particularly when you are starting out, but there is a limit to how much you can reasonably take on. Good planning will enable you to identify those jobs that need to be refused, reassigned elsewhere or recategorized, leaving you free to focus on what is important.

Time stealers imposed from outside

Inevitably, there are some time stealers over which we have little or sometimes even no direct control.

- **Unnecessary meetings** – Calling all and sundry without thought to a meeting is a common fault. Make sure that only the appropriate people attend. When you are invited to a meeting, check the agenda beforehand and if you feel you don't need to be there, make your excuses.

- **Confusion between departments** – A lack of good communication between departments within the company hinders its smooth running and can waste an awful lot of company time – and money. Make sure that all departments are working together for the good of the company as a whole, and encourage and support good communication.

- **Mistakes** – We all make mistakes, so it is important to be patient and understanding when others mess up. Are the mistakes due to poor training or even the lack of it, or something else? If training is needed, make sure it is provided. If there is another cause, take steps to sort it out.

- **Waiting for answers and information** – Establish a system within your own planning routine to chase up information promptly. Make it clear to the person providing the information that you require the response by a certain time or date and that you will chase as soon as it becomes overdue. Be polite, yet reinforce the need for a prompt response.

- **Interruptions** – An inevitable part of working life. While many interruptions are unnecessary and unwanted, others are useful and part and parcel of the job of management. The key here is being able to identify immediately which type it is and to respond in the right way – deal with the interruption there and then, reschedule for attention later, or dismiss it (politely, of course).

Why do business with you?

What makes you different?

The techniques you employ to find and then look after your clients are covered elsewhere in this book, notably in Chapters 7 and 8, but crucial to the whole matter of your business is why your clients choose to do business with you. We know that some clients are purely transactional and buy on price alone, particularly if your business sells fixed item commodities via many outlets. If you are selling services only, the value of the service received will be judged against price as well as benchmarked against service levels delivered by other companies. In each of these cases, you must offer the basic levels of customer care and responsiveness, and deliver on your promise.

However, to keep winning new business and to retain it, you may need to be different, special, exceptional, usual or even predictable. Each of these represents an angle that will be attractive to one of your clients and that will make them choose to do business with you

When you 'open the shop' for business in the morning and set about a new day's trading, for your clients, what you have to offer is coloured by their perception of you and your company. Your reputation and the position you hold visibly in the marketplace are therefore extremely important.

Having a thorough knowledge of your competitors, their products and practices will help you position your business correctly. It will also help ensure you bring in as many clients as possible. Having more clients gives you more opportunity to hunt down that elusive *Big Profit!* So, how do you go about this?

Freedom of choice

Since your clients can choose whether they do business with you or with your rival down the road, there needs to be something special and attractive about your goods and services that pulls them in and persuades them to hand over their money. This is as true of small, high-energy start-ups as it is of large corporate accounts. Your clients need to have clear reasons to part with their funds. So, what can you can do to give them confidence and convert them from being mere potential clients into active purchasing clients?

First, you need to take a close look at the way you and your venture are positioned currently. I don't wish to suggest that you become over-analytical or hire a horde of consultants, but taking a step back from daily business to make a cool analysis of where you are in the marketplace and why, is an invaluable exercise.

Look at what you offer and then put yourself in your clients' place and think about how your goods and services must look from their perspective – think about all your client groups with their many different viewpoints. Do they focus on one particular range of products to the exclusion of others? Do they seem unaware that you also offer certain services? The disparity between their different stances could be very revealing and even offer some surprises. It could also give you ideas for new product creation.

CASE IN POINT

Sarah was running weekend seminars on how to set up a mail order business for greater profit, but this was not why some of the people who attended paid $200 each for their tickets. They were attending the seminar to make money and 'get rich quick', thinking they were going to learn about a franchise for a money-making opportunity. Sarah was simply selling information on how to run a mail order business more efficiently.

When Sarah realized that some of the people were signing up under a misconception, she understood why they thought she was undercharging compared with those of her competitors who were running seminars dedicated to setting up franchise ventures.

Are your clients sufficiently aware of what you are offering in order for you to reap the full rewards from your product or services – and for your clients to feel satisfied with the outcome of their dealings with you and willing to return for repeat business? (See also 'How perceptive is your audience?' in Chapter 8.) Often clients only know your business for the products they buy regularly, unaware of the broader range available. The told/sold matrix in Figure 5.1 allows the sales people to engage with the client and confirm with the client the level of their existing product knowledge, while allowing an opportunity to sell them – or their network – on this broader range.

Products

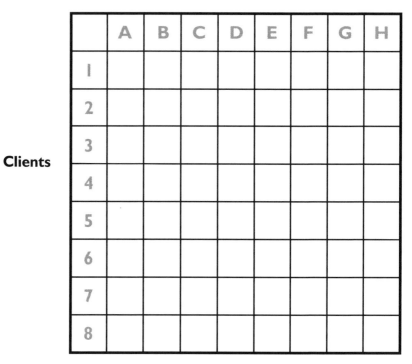

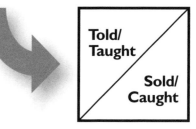

Figure 5.1   The told/sold matrix

Quick questions to assess the market and your place in it

- What am I offering that people are buying?
- Which of my offerings are they not buying?
- What do I have that I want to sell more of?
- Is my perception of what I offer the same as that of my clients?
- If not, how do they differ?

- Who are my clients?

- Do they form a single group, or can I split them up into distinct categories?

- What proportion of my business comes from what proportion of my clients?

- How much do they spend with me on each transaction?

- What is the amount over a year?

- How much new business is referred to me from existing clients?

- How do I reach new clients, communicate with them and access their spending power?

Answering these questions will soon make it clear if you are connecting with the right customer base and which group of clients is the most profitable for you.

An awareness of your clients' budgets can have a huge impact on your business – if you *work* to access them. Find out what money your clients have available to spend and then think how you can make the most of this information. Should you promote certain products above others to certain clients? Can you time your promotions to when they have the most money to spend?

Another benefit arising from this type of exercise is the scope it provides for renewed focus. You cannot be all things to all clients. If you attempt to go down this route, you risk diluting the effectiveness of your services or goods and undermining the business that you have already secured. Accept that some clients will be better served by buying more appropriate products from your competitors and don't waste time and money trying to persuade them otherwise. Look hard at your key strengths and competitive advantages with regard to your principal clients and focus on developing them. If you don't, the result is likely to be a weakening of your efforts accompanied by an unwelcome downturn in profits. It is perfectly feasible to serve a wide general audience with some core product while at the same time serving several lucrative niche markets.

Checking out the competition

It's a jungle out there and jungle law says that in order for you to win a new client, someone else must lose one. Recognizing this is a big step towards grasping why your competitor analysis must be in-depth, data driven, accurate and meaningful! It's the survival of not just the fittest business, but also the one that is in the right place at the right time, and is seen to be so.

Research into the competition serves two purposes. Not only does it help you understand how your company is positioned and perceived within your industry, it also helps you to price your goods correctly within the marketplace. (Product, client and distribution research is dealt with in detail in Chapter 6 and focus groups on page 122, Chapter 8.)

'Mystery shopping'

Don't stint on the collection of data. Get hold of industry magazines, media reviews, competitor and peer group material and information packs. Try your hand at some 'mystery shopping'. Make trips to look around competitors' shops and business operations until you have learned as much as you can about their market share, their client care and staff retention, sales and pricing, marketing, long-term strategy . . . just about every aspect of their businesses in order to build up a full picture of them. Do this for every business you believe to be taking money from both your existing clients and your potential clients. Don't feel too bad about it, it is common practice and one or two of your competitors are probably doing the same to you, and in any case, they/you could take it as a compliment to be seen as a potential threat.

Monitor the competition constantly through press and media reviews and Internet searches on their trading names and brands, so that you can see how they are managing their presence among the marketing forces of your industry. Buy their products, subscribe to their updates, stay in touch with what they do every day.

Commissioned reports

Consider commissioning a report from industry analysts. These are not cheap, but they will save you time and it may be an advantage to have a third party examine close competitors rather than yourself, to avoid arousing any possible antagonism.

Make sure you make the best use of your money by thinking carefully about what you want the report to include, and present the analysts with a list of points. But also be prepared for them to make their own contribution to the focus of the research – you are paying for their expertise after all. Do consider making other uses of the information you commissioned so that you can fully recover your investment cost.

The information you learn about the industry as a whole can also be used as the basis for more successful negotiating with your suppliers. Or it could be used to strengthen your sales presentations by demonstrating a strong awareness of the bigger picture and the issues facing your client.

But don't stop at those businesses in your peer group or those that you consider to be on a par with you. Be aspirational and also look at those who operate in a stratosphere way above you. What can how they operate tell you about why they are so successful? If you are a small regional business, is there a large national one you could study and learn from? It is easier to find out information about large companies than about small ones.

How do you compare with successful businesses?

Once you have assessed your position within your industry, compare your business with those that are successful. Make an objective assessment of these companies' services and products and look at how yours stands up against them. There is great deal to be gained from capitalizing on your competitors' strengths. Look at what they do well, analyse why their product is good or how they achieve their level of service and see how it can be adapted and improved upon in your own business.

Ask yourself the following kinds of questions:

- What is their annual turnover? What are their published profit figures? What about their operating cost/profit ratios?
- What are their staff numbers?
- How do they trade? Shops, mail order, over the counter, on the Internet, at exhibitions, by direct marketing . . . ?
- What is their product development process? How inventive are they? How often do they innovate with new products and offerings?

If you compare favourably with other companies, that's great, but don't rest on your laurels. Someone else will be snapping at your heels in no time, ready to lure your clients away and make off with a slice of your money pie. Be aware of this so that you can spot the predators while they are still circling and before they move in for the kill. Prepare for it by regularly looking for opportunities to reinvent your business, to re-motivate your staff and create new product designs to reconnect with your client base in ways they either don't expect or simply cannot resist.

You are not your business

We have looked at the way your business is perceived by others, but there is another aspect to this that is worth considering. For many of you reading this book, owning family companies or one-person operations, your name IS your business. People do business with YOU, they buy from YOU, they recommend YOU to their contacts and acquaintances. You have built up a reputation for being good at what you do, supplying on time, delivering to budget, and your clients like it that way. Your name is familiar and it makes them feel safe.

Just because you set things up, worked hard, put your name against the bank loan and finally made the whole thing hum, it does not follow that you have to have your name emblazoned across everything from coffee cups to mouse mats. After all your hard work, you might regard a little self promotion as a justifiable reward, but the truth is that it is not an advantage for the business to be wholly identified with you personally. It needs to be able to function without you if need be. You are better off with a business where everything works well regardless of where you are.

There are two issues here. The first is that it is detrimental to the business if it becomes so identified with you that if you do not deal with everything personally orders will be lost. The second is that the business needs to be able to function efficiently whether you are there or not.

Client relationships

Every single contact we have with other people is an opportunity for us to leave our mark and make an impression. Long-lasting client relationships are formed and maintained through good communication and client care at all times, in all our interaction with clients, not just when they are making a transaction.

It's not enough to always be up to date with the latest technology, database or gizmos. Sometimes you win business because you are courteous, kind or friendly, or simply because you are known to care about your clients. After all, if two companies with the same know-how offer the same product at the same price, who wouldn't rather buy from the nice guy rather than the nasty one?

Don't be in it to get rich quick, only chasing after the single *Big Profit!* prize. Your business will be stronger if you have several smaller clients whom you look after well and who remain loyal to you, rather than one big one. (See Chapter 7, where client communication and care are covered in detail.)

Client feedback using information gained from simple methods such as questionnaires or tick-boxes at the bottom of your mailouts can also be used to position your venture within your industry. (See Chapter 7, page 101, where this is dealt with in more detail.

CHAPTER SIX

Pricing

Getting it right

Whatever kind of company you run, you must be selling something or you would not be in business. What you charge for your goods or services has a massive impact on your sales and profit. If your prices are too high, sales will fall quickly, but prices that are too low can cause havoc. Price your goods too cheaply and you risk not having enough cash in the business to sustain its operation. Far more businesses fail because they run out of money than because they run out of ideas, energy or initiative.

My early mentor, Andrew Ferguson, gave me a useful piece of advice: every time a small business gets comfortable with its pricing, it's time to increase by 20% and get uncomfortable again. I have put this into practice many times with many different kinds of businesses over the years and it has nearly always proved to be right. Most small businesses don't charge enough for their goods or services, yet your success or failure is linked directly to correct pricing. As a small-business owner, you may frequently struggle with pricing, finding it hard to judge how far you can push the envelope and raise prices without losing sales. Or you may find it difficult to take an objective view, fully aware of all the work that has gone into your product and its cost, but with little knowledge of the competition's pricing or what the market will stand.

Not too high? Not too low? The obvious answer – though not necessarily the right one – is go for a compromise and opt for a middle range that will work most of the time. Your pricing structure needs to enable you to achieve the largest possible number of sales at the required margin, without turning clients away.

There are five key elements to consider in getting your pricing right:

1 Assessing the market

2 Developing your pricing strategy

3 Price testing

4 Tactics and techniques

5 Increasing your prices.

Assessing the market

Never price your goods or services in isolation – you are not alone in the marketplace, what you offer sits alongside what your competitors are offering. It is not sufficient simply to tot up your production costs, add on your overhead and distribution costs and then slap on a percentage profit. You need to be aware of who your competitors are, what they are selling and at what price, and how your goods or services compare with theirs.

Many of your clients will make a careful comparison of what is available in the marketplace before they buy, so you need to be one step ahead of them. We have already touched on market research in Chapter 5, where knowledge of the competition is important in helping with awareness of how your clients perceive you and why they buy from you rather than from your competitors. In order to get your pricing right, you need to carry out a similar kind of research, but in more detail and targeted towards prices. This kind of research is vital to the success of your venture, but too few business owners take the time to do it.

Gathering the information

Gather 'intelligence' on the core areas of your rivals' offering (including, of course, pricing), client base and distribution for comparison with your own.

Make sure that the information you obtain is detailed and accurate and that the research is carried out systematically. I suggest below the sorts of questions you should be asking yourself, but tailor your research to suit your specific needs.

A thorough understanding of any of these individual areas will have a positive impact on pricing and profit, but knowledge of all of them will give you much greater confidence in your pricing strategy. Use this knowledge to implement new pricing on existing goods or services, or to create brand new products where you see an opportunity for profitable pricing.

Think about carrying out a 'mystery shopping' exercise (see page 68). If you are based in a large city you might be able to do this personally, but in smaller business communities it could arouse antagonism or suspicion, in which case you could hire someone else to do the job for you. You might even want to include your own business in this exercise, in order to find out what an unbiased third party thinks of your operation.

Offering intelligence

The logical place to start is with your offering – the product or service that you sell. Know the offerings of your competitors inside out. If you are a manufacturer, get into the habit of buying your competitors' products to assess them and find out what makes them tick (perhaps literally) by taking them apart and rebuilding them. You can learn a great deal about what makes a product successful, or indeed spot any weaknesses, with this exercise.

- What are the unique features and benefits of your competitors' offerings and how do they differ from yours?
- How successful is your offering in comparison with theirs?
- Given that different customer groups buy different offerings, what factors have enabled your competitors to charge higher prices for certain products and can you do the same?
- How do their prices vary – regionally, by country, by ethnic group, client age group . . . ? Or do they vary according to sales method, such as shop, Internet, barter, cash, credit card . . . ?

- Each product has a life cycle. Where are yours in their individual life cycles: becoming accepted, popular and in demand, in decline, or dying off? If on the decline, what will you do about it?

If you offer services, research in detail the range that your competitors offer. If possible, obtain their promotional literature containing their pricing. When meeting with clients, ask if they have used your competitors and, if so, ask (diplomatically of course) what they thought of their services. Your competitors are unlikely to give you chapter and verse, but they might give you some information that proves useful.

Look at how your services compare with those of your competitors.

- Are there any services that your competitors offer that you don't but should consider?

- Are there any new services you could offer that your customers don't offer?

- But if they don't offer these services, why not? Is there a good reason for this?

Whatever the nature of your offering, every industry has an organization or body that supplies information and promotes its interests. This trade body collects trend data and carries out industry analysis. Contact your trade organization to find out what surveys it has produced that could be of use to you. (I am assuming you are already a member, but if not, why not?)

Client intelligence

Now look at your clients. Look first at your existing clients and track their buying habits, how often they buy, when, at what prices, and track their repeat purchases.

- How big are their purchasing budgets?

- How do they respond to different prices, pricing strategies and discounts?

- Do they respond to loyalty schemes? If not, analyze why, and either adjust or ditch the scheme. How do they respond when you increase prices?

- Would they respond more positively to higher prices if it were clear that your offering had been improved or if there were some other perceived benefit?

- Are you able to charge individual client groups different prices without their being aware of it?

- How price-sensitive is the market?

- Do you have customers who have bought from you in the past but who have not repeated? Do you know why this is? Was it to do with price?

Now look at who else is out there but who is not yet trading with you. Why is this? Perhaps your prices are high and the perception of the value of your offering not clear. Or perhaps they just don't know about you, or are loyal to a competitor. Or is there another reason?

Use client feedback to further your knowledge. Do you have a system that makes it easy for clients to give you feedback? Make sure that it is indeed easy and quick for them to do so, otherwise they won't bother – unless they have a complaint! Make sure that you thank them for having made the effort. See also Chapter 7, page 101, for ideas on how to obtain feedback.

Distribution intelligence

Finally, look at the way your product reaches the marketplace and its onward path to your client.

- Which companies and organizations does your product pass through once it leaves your premises on its way to the end client? (Wholesaler? Distributor? Retailer?)

- Is your current method of distribution the best one for your product?

- Or, could you find a way to do it as well, but more cheaply?

- Or, could you do it better for the same price, or at a higher price but with the goal of fewer returns and complaints?

- Do any of your competitors use the same companies as you? If not, is there a good reason?

- Is there anything you can learn from these companies or can you build a deeper relationship with them?

- If you had a closer relationship with wholesalers and distribution agents, would it lead to a better service, or could you bypass any of them for greater profit?

Developing your pricing strategy – other factors to take into account

The next point is crucial and one that you might think obvious, but many business owners neglect it to some degree. Do you know what it costs to run your business for a day/week/month? Do you know how much it costs to serve a client for half a day? What is the cost to your overhead of holding a one-hour staff meeting? And what about marketing costs, travel, equipment, etc.? When you price your offering, you must be sure you take *everything* into account. If you don't, you will not have an accurate picture of your profit, and your apparently healthy mark-up will soon dwindle in the face of these 'hidden' or indirect costs

Are there any other points that you should consider before working out your pricing strategy? It is important to identify what other factors, either within the business or externally, could influence your pricing decisions – for example, cash flow, operating costs, your position in the market, and your target client group. Unfortunately, more often than not you will find such factors have a restricting rather than liberating effect. For example, you might have shareholders who expect to draw dividends from the venture regularly, damaging your ability to build up a contingency fund of cash. It is also important to take stock of your financial situation, looking not just at your current situation but over the whole year. For example, ask yourself what the effect of increasing your prices would be? If it caused your clients to switch to a competitor, would your business have sufficient funds to weather the storm until you could win back their custom?

Another point to consider is your positioning and the market at which you are aiming. If your market dictates the price, you might have little scope for raising prices or for introducing radically different price points.

Depending upon the nature of your market, where you advertise and how you promote your product, you could compete with yourself by selling two similar products that are differentiated by brand name and packaging. One sells at the lower end of the pricing scale and the other, perhaps of a slightly higher quality, at the higher end. It is better to compete with yourself than to allow one of your competitors to do so!

It is common in many industries (automotive, perfume, haute couture and designer watches are just a few) to imply the credibility or quality of your product simply by charging a higher price than the market average. Your pricing strategy can lead to increased sales or lend greater stability to your product range thanks to the way the market perceives it.

CASE IN POINT Case 1

Nigel is sales director of a ladies clothing company which supplies European department stores. The fabric is made up into garments in factories in the Middle East and the usual policy is to price at cost plus a 60% mark-up. However, all the buyers of the stores to which he sells are keenly aware of his margins and frequently try to barter him down.

To counteract this, he is now very open about his production costs and uses this information as a tool to set a defined lower limit that he will accept. While this does mean that some stores will not match his price requirement, it works effectively with the majority of the buyers to whom he sells.

> **CASE IN POINT** **Case 2**
>
> Jacques and Emilie design and produce earthenware and ceramics. Their factory is staffed by a production team of fourteen and a sales team of two. It has a showroom selling their goods and a public area where refreshments can be purchased while visitors look around the display areas. Jacques and Emilie have fixed and predictable labour costs with a long lease on a fixed rental. They have one retail shop in a particularly affluent area of London and have developed a strong mail order operation.
>
> The difficulty for them in pricing is that if they were to price their items of crockery, dishes, mugs and decorative ware on a cost-plus basis then they would not cover their overheads. By appealing to and selling to a niche group of affluent buyers with their range of country-style themed products they have been able to price upwards steadily, to the point where operational costs and then profits are determined from the carefully monitored revenues through their different outlets (factory shop, the city centre store and the mail order division). Their pricing is therefore driven deliberately by the kudos of what they market and sell. This brand creation then creates demand that further sustains the high pricing.

Price testing – finding the sweet spot

Even armed with a thorough knowledge of the market in which you operate, you may still feel unsure about establishing a pricing structure. But your first attempt at pricing need not be set in stone. Dip a toe in the water and test your prices first. This will enable you to find the optimum price, i.e. the highest price at which you can achieve the maximum number of sales while earning an acceptable level of profit.

In order to find the equivalent of the golfer's sweet spot (the exact spot where the golf club should make contact with the ball for maximum power and accuracy), the canny business owner trials his or her pricing by trying out different price points.

Here's an example of price testing in action.

A mail order company in northern Germany operates with twelve staff and sells several printed information products, how-to products and magazines through its subscriber lists.

They will frequently price test their offerings to distinct postcode and 'personal circumstance' groups. Differentiating among postcode areas is straightforward, but identifying personal circumstance groups is not so easy. It involves looking at people's responses to questionnaires and marketing to them according to lifestyle, interests, age group, hobbies, available savings, etc.

One of the company's clients asked it to price test a monthly stock market investment newsletter. Written by in-house and freelance investment writers, the first edition was designed to gather interest and win subscription revenue. Using direct mail rather than email, the mail order company wrote to a database of 120,000 affluent white-collar professionals who had previously registered an interest in personal finance and investment topics. It price tested at €247, €197 and €97. The price model receiving the best response was €197. It was perceived as being a high enough price to be suggestive of value without being too expensive. Considered alongside the value of the information that would be available each month, the €197 price tag won the day. (Just in case you are wondering, the people who subscribed at the higher test price were not mailed with the other subsets of the price-tested subscription offer.)

For each of the markets in which you operate, you must have an awareness of the pricing that the market will stand.

Underpricing

Underpricing can be just as damaging as overpricing, if not more so. You might find it very difficult to raise the price again if you set it too low initially. Always start with a higher price and you can reduce it gradually while you test the market until you find the right level.

A bizarre effect of underpricing is to reduce sales. Potential clients might be wary if your offering is priced too low, believing that it is too cheap to be any good. And of course, the lower your prices, the lower your profit margins are likely to be. Higher sales might serve to compensate, but this can be dangerous ground. And the detrimental effect of low profits on cash flow is likely to make it even more difficult to sustain the low prices.

Charging too little can also win you the wrong kind of customer, the short-term kind who will soon desert you when they discover that you have to increase prices to enable you to make a reasonable profit.

Tactics and techniques

Once a basic pricing strategy has been established, individual prices can be honed even further for specific purposes, such as to move stock or offer incentives, by making use of psychology and pricing techniques. Review the different pricing techniques that are included here. You might be able to make use of several, although not necessarily at the same time. For example, you might apply bundling with discounts to get great results. On the other hand, you might discover that by giving greater visibility to slow-moving stock and pricing it as an impulse purchase, you can speed up sales.

Discount pricing

The most obvious example is the traditional sale, or end-of-line discount, where prices are lowered because everything must go. Stock moves swiftly in sales because very few of us can resist a bargain, sometimes even when we don't really want the product – as anyone knows who has sale items that they have seldom, if ever, worn languishing in their wardrobe.

Broaden your price range

A range of products at the higher end of the scale should earn you healthy profit, but if you want to secure new customers, you might need to offer some lower priced goods as well. Differences in pricing work well when it is clear which product is for which client group or when a special low price is offered for a period of time, such as a summer promotion of barbecue equipment. The use of discounts can be effective, especially when these are 'once only' or 'special offer' incentives designed to bring people in.

Bundling

Bundling is a pricing tactic with which most business owners will already be familiar as consumers. Several items are sold together for a lower price than if the same number of items were purchased separately. The bundled goods therefore have a higher perceived value. This is a good example of a win–win scenario, in which the customer feels they are getting good value for money, while you benefit from the customer's higher spend. An item offered 'free' when multiple items are bought and 'buy two get one free' are also classic examples of bundling.

Bundled goods normally need to have some form of link between them, such as offering a free pack of snack food when six cans of soft drink are bought, or giving away a lipstick with a women's glossy magazine. Bundling can work well as a seasonal pricing tactic, or as a way of moving stock that is not selling otherwise. It can also be a good way to sell a mix of high- and low- or medium-profit-level products together.

Psychological price barriers

To get a handle on how radically the subtlest of difference in prices can affect sales, think about your own reaction to prices as a consumer. No matter how psychologically aware we are that goods priced at £29.95 are really no cheaper than £30, we still find it less painful to pay the former rather than the latter. Buying two items together for £20 that would sell at £14.95 individually, seems like a great deal. But from the seller's point of view, it might have been difficult to get the customer to part with more than £20 on a casual spend, so it is unlikely they would have bought two separate items at £14.95.

Coins or notes of certain values are easier for us to spend than others. You are no doubt aware of this in your own market currency, but remember that the values change according to the country you are in. I find it relatively easy to spend a £5 or £10 note, yet would seldom dream of using a £50 note.

The psychological effect of this means that goods priced close to £5 or £10 in the UK can be sold with the minimum of fuss. On the other hand, in other countries, it seems easy to spend €50 or $50. If you are selling your offering in another currency, don't just convert it at the spot rate, but think about which value coins or notes people will spend more easily than others.

Impulse purchases

Income in retail outlets can be greatly increased by offering small items at payment points as impulse purchases. These could range from chocolates and novelty gifts to battery packs and sets of screwdrivers, but this technique need not be confined to the traditional retail environment. It can be used wherever it is easy for people to add low-value items to their main orders, such as in mail order catalogues or on the Internet. Online book and audio retailers are adept at informing you that other people who have bought the book or CD that you have just chosen, have also bought X and Y, giving you the opportunity to do the same. It depends upon the market in which you are operating, but these impulse product purchases can add significantly to your profits over and above your core product line.

Bulk purchases

Offering bulk purchase incentives is another way of increasing sales through pricing strategy. You move more stock, but with lower distribution costs since several items are moved in a single transaction. As a result, you can offer a discount in return for the bulk purchase and still make a profit. Another win–win situation.

Increasing your prices

When the time comes to increase prices, which it surely will – you need to earn a decent crust, after all – there are ways to soften the blow and retain goodwill along with those valuable client relationships. Here are a few ideas to help you increase prices without turning people away.

Include a note in your catalogue or on your invoices advising that your current pricing is fixed until a certain date. Or quote a fact that is well known, such as the increasing price of oil, shipping, an increase in interest rates, changes to taxation bands, or a change of business premises, and use this as a lever to raise your own pricing. Each industry sector has factors that you can use to persuade your customers of the need for your increased prices.

Remember that each time you win new business, your new client may have no awareness of your previous pricing. Therefore, you could have several price tiers running parallel. For example, the computer industry has different pricing for large corporate clients for whom it will also tailor computer equipment and software to suit their requirements, and for the home user, for whom the service it offers is less flexible, the equipment standardized and the prices higher.

As a final comment on pricing, I want to emphasize the importance to you and your business of the scope for constant market testing and discussion with your clients. Treat pricing and its dynamics as an exact science and invest in learning more about this aspect of being a business owner. At the very least, work to understand the relationship between pricing, financial forecasting and your ability to make and retain profits within the business.

CHAPTER SEVEN

Communication

Dealing with clients and staff

Good communication is vital for a business to run smoothly and profitably. At the most basic level, the people with whom the small-business owner communicates every day can be divided into two camps – staff and clients. An insight into people's behavioural style can help improve your relationships with these two groups greatly. On the other hand, if you are already communicating well with people instinctively, such insight might crystallize why and help you improve your relationships even further.

Clients and style analysis

You know that clients are your lifeblood. Without them, your business would simply not exist, which is why it makes sense to make use of style analysis in respect of clients and improve your chances of success.

Closing more profitable business by understanding your clients' behavioural style

Have you ever walked away from a purchase simply because you didn't like the salesperson? Have you ever had to turn down an attractive business proposition because you couldn't see yourself working with the person concerned? Does the old maxim, 'we only do business with people we like', ring true for you? If it does, then it follows that you should be able to do more business – and in particular, more *profitable* business – with those people to whom you can relate and with whom you get on well.

Paying special attention to client relationships will soon reap rewards and repay your time and effort handsomely. However, it is not simply a question of old-fashioned good manners and people skills. Awareness within your client relationships plays a major role, as does understanding their behaviour, observing the way they relate to others, and their buying habits.

If this applies to your existing clients, what about the new ones you seek to win over? How should you approach meeting with new clients in order to make the most of your opportunity to secure new business with them?

CASE IN POINT

Jake Robinson runs an importing business out of North Carolina, bringing in silks, table fabrics, wall hangings and decorative art. His goods come from as far afield as Hawaii, Indonesia, Thailand, Guatemala and Honduras. The logistics of the business are relatively simple since all his goods weigh little and are easy to post. Making use of his colourful website and a strong email database, he can do very good business with a relatively low overhead. Yet the venture is not without its troubles.

'When I began just a few years ago, the Internet was still not hugely used and I misunderstood quite a lot of my clients. We were not communicating clearly via email and obviously there was no face-to-face contact. People have different writing styles that reflect their character, which became very evident when I compared different email correspondence. Having recognized this, I now adapt my own style of writing to suit that of my individual clients. We are getting better repeat business and referrals as a result.'

Keep your eyes wide open

Each time a person walks through your office door or speaks with you on the phone you have an opportunity to grow your business. Every time you visit a client in their own environment you have the chance to observe and learn from their behaviour. Most of us miss out on making the most of this kind of opportunity because we don't make a conscious effort to observe the behavioural patterns of our existing or potential clients.

The ability to understand the behaviour of others and to then tailor your own behaviour to suit theirs is a skill that is well worth acquiring. Imagine you are a salesperson for an insurance company and you have a meeting with a client who is keen to purchase £500,000 of life cover from you. The client phones and asks for a meeting and you visit them at home. They make it clear what protection they want and why. They also talk to you about other investments that they might be prepared to make.

The meeting seems to go well until a point at which you feel things become confused, and by the end of the meeting you haven't been able to make a sale. How did the meeting really go? What actually happened? Has this client disappeared for good? You have no idea. But, if you had had an insight into your client's behavioural type, almost certainly you would have been sure of the outcome before the meeting was finished. If the client had been losing interest, you would have been able to 'read' his behaviour, spot the warning signs and take the appropriate action before it was too late.

Other behavioural clues

It is not just what a person says or does or the way they react in certain situations that gives away their behavioural type. Everything about them, from the way they dress to the way they organize their desk (excessively tidy, absent-minded professor mess, or somewhere in between?) gives clues to their true behavioural type. The way a person's home is decorated also tells you about them. So, if you are able to visit a client at home, make the most of this opportunity to help build up your profile of them. Keep your eyes and ears open. Did you note their need for detail? What did they say they wanted in terms of delivery? Were there any specifics? How did they record the information you gave them – traditional pen and paper, or latest techno gadget? Was there any mention of price negotiation or did they accept your quote as final? Were they going away to get a second opinion, or to compare your price with that of a competitor? Maybe they had just ended the meeting to think things through and raise a cheque. There is always at least one client who requires you to see them *at least twice* before they buy anything. If you can spot which of your clients conforms to which type, you will be able to plan your presentations accordingly.

Become your own style-analysis guru

Make style analysis part of your sales toolkit. Study the brief profiles of the different behavioural types that follow here and you will start to observe clear distinctions in their behaviour, revealed in the way they communicate and interact with you. Once you have identified their type, by adapting your behaviour to suit theirs, you will make them feel at ease, confident that they are dealing with someone who is 'on their wavelength', which can only have a beneficial effect on your relationship.

The matrix in Figure 7.1 divides people into four basic types which, for convenience, we call Dominant, Influencing, Steady and Compliant – DISC. Try using the matrix on one of your regular clients. Picture them coming into

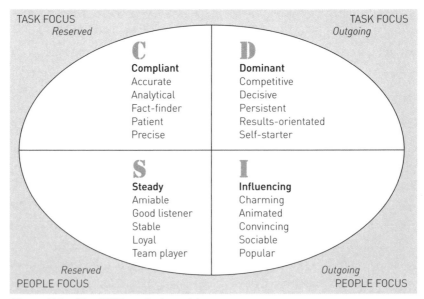

Figure 7.1   The DISC analysis matrix

your office, or you visiting them in their own environment. Think about their behavioural style. What have you noticed about them? Would you say they are on the whole Outgoing or Reserved? Once you have decided this, do you consider them to be more People- or more Task-focused?

Now repeat the exercise with another half a dozen clients. By this time, you might begin to see a pattern emerging.

Now think about yourself. What type are you?

If you see yourself in the S area (lower left) with Steadiness the dominant feature and you are dealing with a someone from the D area (top right), you will probably need to adapt your normal behaviour quite radically in order to deal with them. You may find you are doing this already quite instinctively. But, if this is the case, just being aware of it should help you to develop the relationship even further. By contrast, a client from the I or Influencing area (lower right) is likely to be less confrontational and far easier to deal with.

What does this exercise say about how successful you are at dealing with the different types? Do you find that more of your customers are in one group than another? Does this mean that your behaviour is putting some customers off? Are there any customers whom you have been pursuing, but who have so far proved somewhat reluctant to buy from you? Do you need to change your behaviour towards them, or perhaps think about getting another member of your staff, of a different behavioural type, to deal with them (see 'Match staff member to client', page 93)?

The four behavioural types here are painted with a very broad brush. However, what matters is that you use an appreciation of these four behaviours to understand your clients better and to adapt your own behaviour accordingly in order to develop more fruitful relationships with them. You might also recognize the need to look at your relationships with your clients in a different light.

Putting style analysis to use

You can put your new-found insight to use in all aspects of client relationships. Take a mailing operation, for instance. Instead of the normal 'one size fits all' approach, produce four types of letter, each tailored to appeal to a different behavioural type. Change headings to emphasize one point rather than another. Make the letters of different lengths – shorter for the outgoing and decisive personality, who is likely to be put off by a lengthy read, and longer and more detailed for the reserved and analytical type. A 'PS' at the end of each letter could also be designed to appeal to the different types.

What about meeting venues? Think about the kind of environment that would be most conducive to putting your clients at ease. Would they feel at their most relaxed and amenable on neutral turf in a hotel meeting room, where food and drink can be laid on? Or would they respond better to a meeting at your offices, where they can see your operation in action? How about an informal chat over a round of golf or watching a match?

Match product to client. If you sell financial investments, for example, you will already be aware that people have different attitudes to risk. It follows, therefore, that you can save yourself a great deal of time by matching the product to the client, promoting only those products that most suit their investment behaviour. In addition, limiting the length of your sales presentations by presenting only certain products instead of the whole range, means that those clients with a short attention span are much less likely to switch off or become impatient during your talk.

Communicating with clients

Using style analysis in client communication

Here is a useful guide to communicating with people according to type using the DISC analysis tool. In the business world, it can be put to great use in client communication, although it can equally well be used in many other areas of life. It also suggests how you might deal with each type in a face-to-face meeting.

Recognizing your clients	Communicating with your clients
• D: dominant	
Strong, confident verbal communication	Give factual information
Most forceful spoken style	Allow them to be in charge
Uses direct eye contact	Keep your distance
Points a finger, leans towards you	Demonstrate how other leaders just like them use your products
	Don't waste their time
	They are high-risk-takers
	Only promise what you can deliver
	They are fast decision-makers
• I: influencing	
Animated, friendly, perhaps rambling tone of voice	Provide personal testimonials
Casual conversational style, fairly loud	Make the meeting fun
Smiles a lot, uses expressive gestures and open, demonstrative body language	Be close to them
	Be expressive, use graphic displays
	Use plenty of energy
	They are open to new approaches
	Show them how their purchase will make them look good
• S: steady	
Low voice tone, warm, and detail-oriented	Don't confuse their willingness to buy (i.e. to please you) with satisfaction for your offering
Soft voice, methodical style	Emphasize the guarantee you provide
Small hand gestures	Listen with complete attention
Relaxed, no-emotional style	Don't be confrontational
	Help them to 'feel right' about the investment or purchase
	Avoid interrupting them

▶

- **C: compliant**

Tone of voice is monotone, precise, cool, and can appear aloof	Provide factual information
	Give them evidence to back your claims
Speaks quietly and consider their words carefully	Provide lots of detail and expect them to ask questions
Body language is reserved and controlled, with very few hand gestures	Don't rush their decisions, which can be slow.
Eye contact is direct	Be prepared to cross the 'i's and dot the 't's
	Minimize the risk for them
	Don't invade their space
	Avoid being too personal with them
	They are low-risk-takers

By better understanding your clients' personality type and behaviour, you will find it easier to provide them with the kind of service that will keep them coming back for more and refer you to others.

Match communication method to client

Since the behavioural types of your clients inevitably vary, it follows that the way you communicate with them will produce different results in different scenarios. Here are a few examples of how being aware of your clients' buying behaviour through their behavioural type will help you to close a *Big Profit!* sale.

Mail order

Since they have a preference for buying by post, mail order clients generally respond better to an information pack in the post than to a phone call. But you could try combining the two approaches to improve your chances of a sale or to create scope for upselling product of a related type (that is, getting additional value from a sale). Experiment to see what produces the best results. An offer that sells well via an email newsletter might be a complete disaster sold from a 12-page hard-copy mailout.

Promotional literature and phone

A combination of promotional literature and follow-up phone call is often an effective way of closing a sale. We carry out the recruiting for our seminars in this way and find that most people respond well to the phone call we make following their receipt of our literature. Some people will even sign up during the call. They are a more interactive behavioural type, whereas those who sign up by post, email or fax are more analytical, preferring the security of buying in hard-copy form.

If you are selling something at a distance rather than face-to-face, you don't have the chance to interact personally with the client. Your sales letter or advert therefore has to do the job for you, so clearly it is important to get it right. If you are not confident about your writing skills, take advice on how to write good, snappy copy, or hire someone who can do it for you.

Match staff member to client

We've already said that, in general, people prefer to do business with people they like. It just makes the whole transaction more pleasurable for both parties. It is inevitable that you will get on better with some clients than others. Think about those clients with whom you don't get on quite so well, the ones 'just beyond the comfort zone'. By being aware of their behavioural type, you might be able to adapt your own behaviour sufficiently in order to have a good business relationship with them. On the other hand, another member of your team might be able to strike up a better relationship with them than you, so perhaps you should step back and allow them to take over this client. Make the most of the different personality types within your team and allow clients to gravitate towards their preferred staff contact.

CASE IN POINT

Dirk operates a furniture-finding service specializing in French antiques. His six staff help him to source pieces from dealers, auctioneers, showrooms and private sales. When a new client makes an enquiry, Dirk allocates them to one of the six on his team. He does this based on his knowledge of his employees' style and personality and his assessment of the client's style. As a result, because his clients feel they are working with someone who is 'on the same wavelength', they feel relaxed and happy. Thanks to this, Dirk and his team get rave reviews from enthusiastic clients and a good deal of referral business.

First impressions

Think about the impression your clients receive on their first contact with your business. Is your logo eye-catching? Is the company name clear? Is your headed paper of good quality? How do staff answer the telephone? First impressions are hugely important. They can turn a client away instantly, or draw them in. What about your website? How welcoming and user-friendly is it? A simple but useful exercise to help you get your 'welcome' right is to choose ten websites at random from any of those promoted to you each day. Log on and look for anything on the site that might be termed a warm welcome. Too many sites give an off-putting message, making it clear they assume you have only logged on in order to buy from them. Check their welcome pages. Why do you think this one is inviting and that one is indifferent? Evaluate why you react as you do to these sites. Have you learned anything that can be applied to your own website, the recorded message on your voicemail, or the way you write your compliment slips?

Put yourself in your clients' position. How recognized and special would you feel contacting your company? It takes just moments to make someone feel welcome, yet the rewards that these personal touches bring will repay you many times over with repeat business and enhanced profitability.

More client care = more *Big Profit!*

'Client care' is a phrase that trips off the tongue, but there is surprisingly little awareness of just what it involves and why it drives profits for those who do it well. Looking after your clients and expressing your appreciation for their custom builds and strengthens client relationships. Building relationships in turn strengthens your client network. Strong networks will *always* bring you more business, and not only more, but better-quality business. Better-quality business is *Big Profit!* business. That's the kind of profit that will enable your business, and therefore you, to become more successful.

Depending upon who you talk to – client-care managers, service gurus, PR agents – there are any number of golden rules that are crucial to successful customer service. However, being sent on your way with, 'Thank you for having chosen to use MegaBucks services, please call again', ringing insincerely in your ears, simply because this phrase is set out in the client-care handbook, can backfire.

'Real' customer service should amaze the client, catch them unawares and then surprise them again. It can be as simple as doing something for some-one without being asked. Or, at the opposite end of the scale, it could be making a delivery with such efficiency, style and panache that the client is left in awe. Then again, it could be the client knowing that help and com-plete efficiency are just a phone call away.

CASE IN POINT **Case 1**

Collecting my car from its service after another 10,000 kilometres, it was great to find that it had been cleaned both outside and inside . . . but the clincher was the small bag of sweets placed on the arm-rests and the fresh bottles of mineral water in the cup holders. Simple, but so effective. No wonder we wouldn't take our cars any-where else.

> **CASE IN POINT** | **Case 2**
>
> Dining with friends in a new restaurant for the first time, it was wonderful to be served with canapés while we made our choices from the menu. Having ordered our food, the head waiter then talked us through the wine list, making it all the more interesting and personal as he was able to talk from first-hand experience following his recent familiarization tour of the vineyards.

> **CASE IN POINT** | **Case 3**
>
> Receiving a Christmas card from the shopkeeper of a small store ten months after having first shopped with him was nice, and finding a handwritten note inside was rare, but referring to something I had commented on months ago was a true feat of memory and client interest. I am sure to keep going back and am equally likely to refer friends and family to the store. Why? Because, the shopkeeper made an effort to show he valued my custom long after it (in theory) ceased to be necessary.

The cost of client care – money well spent

It is a fact that it costs less to look after a client who is already buying from you than to win a new customer. But to make the point more forcefully, I'll be a bit more blatant.

You can spend money wisely on looking after a client whose custom has proved profitable in the past, and who is likely to continue spending money with you at a decent margin in the future. Or, you can invest money in bringing in new clients, hoping that they will grow to become profitable, but this is a gamble.

I know I am stretching the point somewhat but we are talking about *your* money. How do you feel about wasting it? Imagine tearing it up, setting light to it and throwing it out of the car window. Do you get the picture? When you invest money in buying a new mailing list, promoting a theatre production, buying a table at the local business black-tie dinner, or any other venture designed to bring in new clients, you are unable to guarantee the results.

By contrast, when you spend £100 thanking an existing client – whose spending behaviour with *your* business you already understand and can monitor closely – you can better predict the return on your investment.

How should you go about expressing your appreciation?

It could be with a simple and sincere handwritten 'thank you' card or a box of chocolates, or drinks delivered to a client's office or home address. The legal firm we use is always inviting us to race meetings, and I know a consultant who invites his clients and suppliers to paintball or go-karting weekends. But thanks can equally well be expressed on a much smaller scale with a small but high-quality gift, such as luxury toiletries, which the client would not normally buy for themselves.

If you respond well to such behaviour when you are a client, it follows that your clients will respond well when you make the effort to show that you value their custom. Knowing we are important makes us feel special and cared for and motivates us to remain loyal clients, creating a bond of goodwill that is invaluable. But don't overdo it – don't be overly chummy or insincere. Someone you have met only once at an exhibition several years ago and who has not since contacted you is unlikely to change their mind about doing business with you simply because you send them a Christmas card every year.

Here are some examples of the 'old-fashioned' personal touches that many business owners neglect:

- 'Thank you' notes when something merits one.
- A handwritten compliment slip.
- Letters written by a person rather than churned out by a computer.
- Small gifts sent spontaneously with an order, simply to show you value their custom.

- Remembering personal details such as a birthday, the name of a family member, where your client likes to go on holiday . . .
- The sharing of a personal client story in a mailed catalogue or an e-zine newsletter.
- Cherish your suppliers. Acknowledge and thank them for the important role they play in your business success.

The importance of personal recognition

When you look at a group photograph of the sports team in which you play, who do you look for first? Yourself. Narcissistic? Perhaps. But most people would do the same. It follows therefore, that, apart from celebrities travelling incognito, most people like to be recognized. Make an effort to recognize your clients, even the ones who are not regular. If you are not good at matching faces with names, try to fix upon something about them that is quirky or different and match it mentally with their name. Hopefully, the quirk will then trigger the right name the next time you meet them.

Personal recognition is probably the simplest example of client care after saying 'thank you', and what's more, it costs absolutely nothing.

CASE IN POINT

'Hello! You're one of our Golden Oldies!'

This was the greeting I received when I called my favourite business magazine to report on our change of office address. The editor immediately recognized me as being one of his long-term subscribers and I immediately felt that the cost of the annual subscription was well worth it.

Make your client care something special

I mentioned earlier that 'real' customer service should amaze the client, catch them unawares. Here are some suggestions of things that you might do to pleasantly surprise your clients and to convince them that they want to keep giving you their business.

- Let your clients know you enjoy working with them and for them.

- Admit to a mistake when you have made one, so that your clients know you are honest and human.

- Do something positive for them that they could never anticipate.

- Once the sale is made and the money is in your bank, don't just abandon your clients. Help them to get the best out of what they have bought from you with after-sales care.

- Be aware of what your competitors are doing in terms of client care – and do every single little thing that you can to get ahead of them.

- It is normal to want to impress your clients but not to let them sense that they might have impressed you. Don't be afraid to admit to a client that they have impressed you. It will make them feel good and better disposed towards you.

> ### CASE IN POINT Resourcefulness and customer care
>
> David and Louise have a team of fifteen people hiring out construction power tools, vehicles and excavators, often at short notice, to businesses whose equipment has failed.
>
> While they do not have a huge stock of tools and vehicles themselves, they have a policy of working closely with other companies and ensuring the right equipment is sourced as quickly as possible. Their business USP, or unique selling proposition, is that if they cannot supply it themselves, they will source the equipment for the client. It is much better to hear, 'We don't have one at the moment, but let me find out how quickly we can have one on site for you', than it is to be given the simple negative response that would be more common. Their awareness of the importance of customer care ensures repeat business from existing clients and the addition of new ones as word spreads.
>
> David and Louise charge slightly more than their competitors, but their customer care more than compensates for this as far as their clients are concerned.

Don't overlook anyone

Apart from those clients who buy from you directly, who else should you be thanking for believing in you and having been loyal, and for referring you on to others? What about those who have championed your company, even if they have not bought from you?

Who stands behind you and cheers you on – no matter how quietly?

What about the client who introduced you to a member of his extended family for new business last month?

What great opportunities have resulted from hosting a social evening or weekday lunch event for your suppliers? Have you thanked them for attending and for the referrals they gave you as a result?

Make a note of these people now and schedule in your diary the calls and the meetings you need to set up in order to start showing your appreciation.

Getting client feedback

Feedback is good for business. You need to know what people really think about your goods and services in order to keep your market position. There are a number of ways of going about this. Here are a few ideas.

In printed form

Customer satisfaction surveys are one way of getting feedback, although if carried out in isolation they can be a waste of time. If you decide to try a survey, think carefully about the kind of information you want to know and set your questions accordingly. The questions can be slanted to cover any aspect you choose – level of service, pricing, distribution, buying habits and so on. You might ask your customers about the kinds of goods or services they buy, or want to buy but cannot source, any difficulties that they have experienced, what performs well for them . . . Make sure you also give them the opportunity to comment on anything they feel is important that you have not covered in your questions. By way of thanks and incentive, offer them free copies of the report that you compile as a result (assuming it is suitable to do so) – they might find your analysis useful too. Or enter all the surveys in a prize draw.

In addition to the questionnaire, where all clients receive the same document or interview questions, printed feedback can be gathered on a more ad hoc basis using small tick-box survey cards left at the point of transaction. The client can be asked to complete the card and deposit it in an adjacent collection box or to hand it to a member of staff. Hotels often leave such questionnaires in bedrooms and request them at checkout. Worried at the thought of the kind of feedback they might receive, small-business owners might fear doing this, but they are missing out on a valuable opportunity to learn what their clients think of them.

By phone

A distribution company might phone a client after making a delivery and ask specific questions as to what might have been done better. Make sure that the person making the calls has knowledge of the product or service. For example, if you sell fishing equipment, make sure that the caller is familiar with the range of equipment you sell and understands how it is used. Even better, recruit people who are passionate about fishing. Your clients are not likely to give you the detailed feedback you need if they feel the person to whom they are talking has no knowledge of the product. This is just a waste of staff time and your money.

It is important to get the timing of your phone calls right. When will your clients have the time to take the call? Lunchtime, afternoon, early evening? Do you call them at work or at home? If you are not sure, make some trial calls to test the kind of response you receive. When you make your first transaction with a client, ask them when the best time would be to call, should you ever need to do so.

By post

Why should someone give up their time to complete your survey? Think of what incentives you can use to persuade them to respond, regardless of how angry or frustrated with your business they may be. A pre-paid return envelope might help, and what about entering their survey in a prize draw? Is there some other incentive that would encourage them to respond to your questions?

Automated email response system

These are easy to set up, but much will depend upon how much you know about your clients' ease of access to the Internet. Do they have home or work access to the Internet? Do they have permanent broadband access? When do they tend to use the Internet – at work or at home? How long do they stay online? Are they familiar with how to complete an online questionnaire?

Informal events

Yet another route is to invite clients to an unstructured event held in an informal atmosphere designed to encourage them to speak freely. Staff from the company can meet with them and discuss trade and the perception of care and attention to detail given to their orders.

Get something positive out of dealing with unhappy clients

Dealing with upset and angry customers is not something most of us would choose to do, but when things go wrong, clients have to be faced. If you have to speak to a disgruntled client, adopt a positive attitude and do your best to draw some benefit from what has happened. View it as an opportunity to learn what you might do differently next time.

Here are some tips to get the most out of dealing with a complaint:

- Bite the bullet and get in touch with your client quickly, but before taking any action just listen and allow them to have their say. What is the cause of their complaint and does anything else lie behind it?

- Apologize and make sure they realize that your apology is sincere. An insincere apology could damage your business just as much, if not more, than the cause for the complaint. Provided you understand your role in the business then you should not have an issue with being honest about an apology. Your reputation is the business, and as its figurehead you should be open to criticism and be willing to keep learning and improving.

- If appropriate, and if it is what they want, offer your client a prompt refund, discount or money incentive. If you don't believe it is right to give them a refund, then hold your ground or let a client-focused colleague take over the discussions.

- Demonstrate to your client, if it is true, that their experience was a one-off – a mistake or an unusual situation. Help them to see just how unusual it really was.

- Give your client the chance to suggest how you could do things better or differently next time.

- Thank your client for having highlighted an issue of which you were unaware and having given you the chance to rectify it.

- Find out what would be required by your client to have them overlook your mistake and keep trading with you.

- Look for something that makes it worthwhile to have received and handled the complaint. Perhaps it will present you with the opportunity to improve your staff's skills. Or perhaps the new system that is implemented as a result of the complaint might also prove to be a source of extra revenue for you.

- Be available. Don't hide behind your staff, your status or your voicemail. Face the client and give them the chance to see that you really do care about their concerns. They may only want the opportunity to vent their frustration and air their grievances to the person at the top. Ten or twenty minutes of discomfort is a small price to pay for retaining the custom of a loyal client.

- Finally, be realistic and acknowledge that you cannot please everyone. You will also sleep better when you realize that sometimes there is a limit to what can be done to rectify mistakes. If you have done all you can, you have done your best, even though a client may not appreciate or believe it.

CASE IN POINT

Neil had called his supplier four times, wanting to speak to the owner whom he had met at a seminar. On each occasion the call was taken by a different person, who said they would pass the message on. Finally, Neil did manage to leave a brief message on the owner's voicemail. The owner listened to the message intending to take action later. But, busy as ever, time went by until in his mind he confused listening to the message with actually dealing with it. After several weeks of trying to get in touch, Neil gave up. When he later met another client who'd had the same experience, they compared notes and spent several minutes complaining to each other about the apparently elusive owner.

Neil was already unhappy with the situation, but when he realized he was not alone in his dissatisfaction, his sense of annoyance began to escalate. He called the business and insisted on offloading all his anger and frustration on to the administrator who handled the call. Since Neil made the administrator fully aware of just how unhappy he was, the administrator located the owner and insisted that Neil be called back. The owner duly made the call and was subjected to twenty minutes of Neil's wrath.

Initially, all Neil had wanted was to talk to the owner. Then, as his annoyance mounted with each unsuccessful call, he wanted someone to whom he could air his grievance about the elusiveness of the owner and the lack of communication within the company.

A week later, Neil and the owner met up once more face-to-face and spoke together for some time. The following morning, the owner gathered his team together and set about installing the systems that would make sure this could not happen again. Within just a few months, Neil was trading with the owner once more and had spread the word among other clients that the owner really did care about his customers and was prepared to listen to them when things went wrong.

As far at the owner was concerned, he realized that he could keep his profits healthy simply by looking after his existing clients better. Any new revenue from any new systems implemented would be an added bonus.

And the moral of this story? There are several:

- Be willing to learn from a client's concerns.
- Install any systems necessary to prevent a recurrence of the mistake or situation that gave rise to it.
- When a client wants to be heard, make it possible for them.
- Lead by example. If you, as the boss, show your willingness to get involved with client care, your staff can only follow suit.
- As the owner, be prepared to shoulder the responsibility for a mistake or problem before delegating its solution.

Staff and style analysis

Communication with staff is an equally important area. Staff are fundamental to the smooth running of your business. Any conflict, misunderstandings or unhappiness with or among your staff will not add to the bottom line, but are much more likely to harm it.

Applying style analysis to staff selection and recruitment

The traditional recruitment route involves writing a job specification and placing an advert in the press or with a recruitment agency. It is a time-consuming business that frequently involves a number of staff and impacts directly on your overhead. It can also achieve imperfect results. Despite sifting through CVs carefully and calling candidates for interview to assess their qualifications, work history and personality, it is still easy to make the wrong choice.

The DISC analysis system described on page 88 can also be used to great effect in recruitment. By taking into account candidates' natural behavioural style as well as their attitude and values, an employer will gain an insight into how they view the world. It will also help them identify areas in which the applicant is likely to excel, spot potential strengths which could be developed, and assess how the candidate would fit in with the existing staff.

Draw up a profile of the position to be filled, detailing the professional skills and qualifications needed as well as the tasks involved in the job. Those candidates who match the required criteria can be invited for interview.

If it is an administrative position that is to be filled, complete a job profile that details what tasks the job involves and with which other members of staff the administrator will interact. This will give you a clear idea of how each candidate is likely to fare in the role and what training they might require in terms of handling email, stock control, client contact, etc.

Contingency plan

Despite your best efforts to recruit the right person, it is still easy to make the wrong choice, which can have a detrimental effect on your bottom line.

Our new staff are now employed with an initial probationary period so that we can be sure that we like each other and can work together before a contract for permanent employment is signed. If you are not already doing so, try employing people on a probationary-period basis. It will enable both parties to opt out without rancour at the end of the set time. However, bear in mind that some people take longer than others to feel accepted or to begin working effectively as part of an existing team.

CASE IN POINT

Mike ran a small print and design service from a rented unit on the edge of his town. Employing four staff and enjoying steady growth, he decided to recruit a financial controller to make sense of the paperwork, deal with creditors, manage the bank accounts and update Mike on financial trends. After a couple of months the company's bank balance was still healthy, but Mike began hearing whispers of discontent from his suppliers.

It transpired that Mike's new financial controller was being curt or even rude on the phone, promising suppliers payment only when he was ready. Mike had prided himself on paying his company's bills within 30 days. Unfortunately, his new employee, believing that delaying payment was helping to increase the bank balance, was in the process of destroying the valuable relationships Mike had painstakingly built up. Unsurprisingly, Mike decided that he and his financial controller should part company immediately, but thanks to the contractual probationary period, the matter was handled without too much upset.

Conflict within

The ideal staff team is one in which knowledge and skills are dovetailed so that a person whose strengths lie in one area is paired with someone who has expertise in another. However, it is not just job skills that need to be a good fit; personalities need to work well together too, and the more people you employ, the bigger the risk of a personality clash or conflict somewhere within your team. If matching staff with clients in terms of compatibility of temperament pays dividends, the same certainly applies to your staff.

> **CASE IN POINT**
>
> When interviewing for a new sales administrator, Jamie saw the ability to think independently and a flair for sales in the forceful character of one of the candidates, as strengths that would be a boon to the department. Unfortunately, Jamie's staff felt the new administrator was simply arrogant and unpleasant and his presence in the department began to cause problems. The result was that Jamie had to lose the new staff member in order not to have resentment and unrest build up within the rest of the team. However, sometimes the arrival of a challenging new employee can act as a catalyst, causing other staff members to raise their own game and work more effectively.

Communicating with staff

Once you have recruited the right people for your team, you must ensure that you, as the business owner, communicate with them effectively. Business owners used to working alone and keeping everything in their head may need to pay special attention to this point.

- I have already made this point a couple of times, but employing staff frees up your time by enabling you to delegate work. Make sure you delegate tasks to those staff members who can be held accountable. Delegating to someone who will not shoulder responsibility for the task is asking for trouble. Allowing others to take on some of your tasks, regardless of their understanding of the business as a whole, will eliminate much worry and stress. If your employees can look after clients and fully deliver the expected level of service, your business becomes stronger precisely because you no longer need to perform all the tasks.

- Once you have delegated the tasks, make it clear that you will step in to do a regular or random assessment of results and performance.

- Make sure there is a link between effort and reward, perhaps via a bonus, a commission or another incentive-linked assessment of their work – but make sure the link is clear. The reward should act as an incentive without being overly generous. Being too liberal with rewards can backfire if staff start taking the rewards for granted, and can also make it difficult to continue coming up with new and effective incentives.

- Make clear what is expected of staff in terms of output or results, such as what sales are budgeted to be achieved, or what is the target for the number of units to be manufactured over a certain period of time.

- Establish a fixed reporting system and schedule, whether daily, weekly or monthly. Make sure that you, as the business owner, receive regular feedback from the system. This could be face to face from a line manager, from a client, or by telephone, email, etc.

- Keep staff informed of the bigger picture and how the company is performing as a whole. People like to be involved and feel trusted. I am sure that communicating regularly to your staff what is happening in the business plays a vital part in its long-term growth and survival. See also Chapter 2 for advice on managing change and implementing new strategies.

Beware your inner control freak!

The *Small Business* owner looking for *Big Profit!* needs to learn to let go of established or traditional ideas about how people should work. Some staff may respond well to having strict working methods imposed on them, but you should be flexible enough to allow those who find such strictures frustrating and limiting to choose their preferred working method. Provided that they can still achieve the required results and their method does not interfere with the systems that are vital to the smooth running of the company, the result should be a happier and more contented workforce.

CASE IN POINT

For some time, Mary felt that one of her administrators was not performing well enough and so tried to keep a close eye on his work. She insisted that he attend a training programme which would be of benefit to him even though the administrator disliked the idea intensely. As a result, he felt resentful and did not enjoy the course, getting little benefit out of it.

A better plan might have been to suggest that the administrator choose a course that interested him and ask him to report back on his progress. When Mary did finally adopt this approach, a number of her staff registered for different courses of their choice, and, provided Mary felt the courses were appropriate, she was happy for them to go ahead. The result was beneficial to all parties. The staff members improved their skills and enjoyed learning about subject areas that interested them. They worked more efficiently, morale was raised and the whole company benefited as a result.

Mary realized that the real issue had been that she had not allowed her administrator to get on with his work in the way that he preferred and had imposed her own working method on him. Once she made it clear what was expected, but was less concerned with how he went about it, the administrator was able to fulfil his role well, reporting on the trends and data required. Mary, as the employer, had simply needed to demonstrate that she had confidence in her employee's abilities and leave him alone to get on with the job.

Staff care

If you employ staff, although you are providing them with a means to earn a living, you are also doing so for your own benefit. They should make your life easier and your business more productive. When you bring people on to the payroll they should either contribute directly to the bottom line or release another person to do so. If not, you are simply adding another ball to the ones that you are already juggling in the air, building up towards an expensive crash when one or more drops to the ground as your business overheads become punishing.

Apart from the desire to treat your staff well on the grounds of simple decency, from a less altruistic point of view, if you treat them well, they will be happier and in turn more productive. You therefore have every reason to do your best to make your relationship with your staff a win–win situation, one in which you benefit from their work and your staff lead happy and ful-filled working lives.

Are you happy with your staff and are they happy working for you? Are they working efficiently? Are there any changes you could make that would benefit both parties? Here are a few ideas to consider and perhaps they will prompt you to think about others appropriate to your venture.

- Do all staff need to work from your existing premises? Could some work equally well from home with the right equipment?
- Do staff need to work the traditional 9to5, five days a week, or will the results be the same if you introduce flexible working hours? Or might they even be improved because staff are more motivated when working hours to suit their individual circumstances?
- How many people need to be at your regular internal meetings, and should you hold these less or more frequently?
- Can each person or team be encouraged to manage and report on their own monthly Profit and Loss account, creating new gains and reducing overheads, and giving them increased job satisfaction from more respon-sibility?

- Can the interview process be broadened to involve the applicant's potential work colleagues, to help reduce the opportunity for personality conflict and keep staff turnover to a minimum?

- Do you have the scope to change the structure of your salary and bonus package? Not everyone wants a simple fixed salary. Some might prefer a mix of fixed salary and annual profit-sharing, whereas others might be motivated by access to sales commissions, stock options, productivity bonuses or rewards for achievement of self-prescribed goals.

Be open to new ideas

Give all levels of your staff scope to contribute new ideas in working practice, from the office junior upwards (after all, everyone has to start somewhere and you might be nurturing the next rising star). Be ready to take their ideas on board, adapting them to suit your own purposes if necessary.

CASE IN POINT

After Pete had spoken at a conference for travel agents he was approached by a young woman asking for holiday employment before she went back to college. Sophie joined Pete's business organizing tailor-made holiday packages for tour operators and travel agents for just eight weeks. She had no qualms about using Pete's existing systems, but brought with her lots of new ideas. She was happy picking up a phone and talking to travel agents, hotels, charter airlines, etc. Relaxed in her style and enthusiastic about the product range, she achieved excellent results, even outstripping a full-time employee. Sophie went back to college as scheduled, but Pete decided to incorporate some aspects of her working methods into the daily structure. She continues to work in Pete's business during her vacations, which helps support her through college.

I am convinced that allowing staff to demonstrate their abilities to the full and being open to any innovations that they might have, contributes significantly to your profitability. Providing an environment of trust and support for new ideas is part of your role as the driving force behind your ever-changing *Small Business, Big Profit!* enterprise.

CHAPTER EIGHT

Marketing matters

Getting the right message out there

Marketing is generally defined as the raising of profile, the gathering of attention to your product or cause. But the definition that I most enjoy is:

'The art and science of getting potential clients to understand what you and your business do, and being clear about the benefits of your activities, for **them**.'

Marketing is possibly the least understood aspect of many small businesses, yet once grasped, it is the key to *Big Profit!* results. I am convinced that if more business owners were to acknowledge and act on this, they would enjoy greater success. I have seen small businesses fail time and again, both as a small business adviser and as an operator of ventures within my own markets. It hurts to be so close and see this happen. These businesses frequently have a great product, a fabulous new idea or a fresh approach to a standard challenge. They are almost surprised when their offering is not snapped up in quantity by a grateful public and they go out of business quickly. Why?

Because their potential audience did not know enough about them to trade with them in the numbers necessary for their business to survive and prosper. Whatever the nature of your own business, make it a priority to market it daily and with commitment. Your audience will change, grow and be replaced. Provided you stay in touch with such changes, you can continue to put your message in front of the right people at the right time and attract them to your business.

But marketing is not something you should do on an ad hoc basis, just when you have the time or spare cash. Successful marketing needs momentum – it needs to be an ongoing process that is monitored and adjusted according to the needs of the market. This is probably why so many well-intentioned business owners tend to overlook it, concentrating instead on the basic operational aspects of their venture and realizing only too late that no one seems to know what they do or how well they do it. The time to recognise the importance of marketing is not just as the bank is pulling the financial rug from beneath your feet.

My aim in this chapter is not to explain the many different marketing techniques, but rather to get you thinking specifically and strategically, rather than generally, about what you wish to achieve so that you can get the most out of your marketing effort.

Your marketing activities should be affordable and foolproof and, once established, able to be duplicated easily and with minimum effort by you and your team. But, at this stage, you don't need a big chunky textbook or an MBA in marketing to do it successfully! You just need a well-thought-out plan, targeting the right areas of your business and implemented using the appropriate methods, that will make sure people hear about what you do and want to buy into you, your products and your ideas.

How can marketing help you?

I'll answer this with another question: What do you want to achieve from your marketing activity? This is a key question and not as simple to answer as you might at first think. Most business owners would answer immediately that they want to see an increase in profitability, or that they want to develop the business – but isn't this every business owner's goal, regardless of whether they do any effective and successful marketing? Rather than go about it in a vague 'we've got some spare cash, let's advertise the business' kind of way, it is important that you make your marketing specific in order to spend your time and money most effectively. If you want to bring in more income or grow the business, you must first decide which areas of it you should target.

The first step is to draw up a marketing plan in which funds are allocated to specific products and activities in specific periods. This is a must to make sure that the money is spent as wisely as possible. A plan with both time-bound and project-based spending targets can have a profound effect on the business. It also has the advantage of compelling you and your staff to take personal responsibility for how the money is used.

The second step is to make an objective assessment of the effect that marketing could have in each sector of your business. Which areas would be likely to produce the most response, and what level of response would you be looking for? It might be difficult to judge if you are approaching this for the first time, but try to be realistic about what you might actually achieve.

The third step is to look at the different kinds of approaches that you could use and decide which of them might be expected to gain you the best results, and why.

Let's look briefly at the two main types of marketing The first is **profile raising or brand publicity**. This simply means getting your name out there in the marketplace and involves making the most of public relations (PR) opportunities by placing adverts, linking with websites of related businesses, sponsoring relevant events or charities and generally educating the world about what you do and how you might do it for them. PR is a cost-effective medium compared with advertising, yet it is used effectively only by a minority of businesses. Talking about your business in the right places and to the right people (especially journalists with column inches to fill) creates editorial copy which carries more credibility than adverts for those who see it.

The second type of marketing is the **client-specific approach**. Here your aim is to reach individual clients by such activities as personalized email and written correspondence, or holding an event especially for one client or a small group of prospective clients, or sector-specific seminar invitations. Permission-based marketing is about creating situations where your potential clients are proactive, asking you to get in touch and provide them with information. Or the marketing might be set up so that they ask to do a 'road test' of your product, but at a time and location that are convenient for you.

Whatever methods you choose, one thing is certain. 'Time poverty' has become one of the biggest concepts to affect marketing today. Adverts are shorter and more focused and now TV must compete with other media such as the Internet. People are not so much interested in knowing what is available, as in knowing what is available that is suitable for them. They also want to know that it can be provided in such a way that it doesn't take up too much of their time or cause them too much inconvenience.

Budgeting for your marketing activity

Clearly, your marketing plan needs money, but before you work out what you can afford to spend, you need to know how much you are already spending on marketing. Perhaps you think it is next to nothing, but those small-value invoices can mount up, and the boundary between what constitutes marketing and what constitutes other kinds of business activity can be blurred. Does a hospitality lunch or an overseas trip for preferred suppliers represent marketing or is it relationship-building – and what is the difference? Is the expenditure on office stationery bearing your brand and message a marketing expenditure or an office operations spend? You'll need to decide what counts as marketing and what does not.

Whereas some business owners simply allocate a fixed percentage of revenues to marketing spend, others adopt a more flexible approach. If you believe you have judged the amount of your previous spend correctly, you will probably continue to allocate funds at the same level. But how much of last year's spend was planned properly?

Where does the money go – on existing or potential clients?

Differentiating between potential and existing clients is crucial when considering your marketing spend. In most firms, the majority of the marketing budget is spent on potential clients. This is usually because mass marketing tools such as advertising, and especially advertising in print, tend to be vastly more expensive than other methods. Yet research has shown that it costs between five and ten times more to win business from new clients than it does to get repeat business from existing clients. In fact, it's at least twice as easy to win back business from ex-clients (those who traded with you previously but then went elsewhere) than from those who have never bought from you before. So, doesn't it make sense to ensure that you devote the majority of your marketing spend to winning more business from existing clients, while finding more economical ways of maintaining and building your profile with prospective clients?

Calculating the lifetime value (LTV) of your clients

This is a useful exercise, which we have already touched upon in Chapter 3. Calculating the total amount of money that existing clients are likely to spend with you during the whole of your trading relationship, or even just over a certain period of time, will give you great insight into how much you should spend on marketing activity directed at retaining them. Many business owners don't do this exercise, but if they did, they would make much better use of their marketing funds.

CASE IN POINT   **Case 1**

Beautiful Bathrooms manufactures top-of-the-range bathroom suites and sells them to bathroom retail outlets all over the country at £4,000 each. It has been supplying one such outlet, Clean and Sparkly, for ten years. Clean and Sparkly is located in a relatively poor inner city area and only sells three top-of-the-range suites at £8,000 each over roughly five years. Knowing this allows Beautiful Bathrooms to calculate how much it should allocate to advertising in this area. It knows that if it looks after Clean and Sparkly as a client, it can tap into a potential revenue of around 3 × £8,000 = £24,000 every five years. At the same time, this figure gives Beautiful Bathrooms valuable demographic information on what sales prices the market in that area will stand.

> **CASE IN POINT** | **Case 2**
>
> Molly's Mart is a chain of supermarkets with 30 stores in the south west of the country. Molly's tracks the spending patterns of its customers very precisely through its loyalty card scheme and so knows that the Giles family living in the largest town in the region spend £240 a week on food and £100 a week on petrol – in total around £18,000 a year. Molly's therefore knows just how much of its marketing and promotional budgets it can afford to spend per year on reaching that family, and thousands like it, to persuade them to keep shopping at Molly's. Similarly, Molly's can also work out how much it can afford to offer in incentives by way of its loyalty cards, seasonal discounts and other such schemes.

What are the lifetime value figures for one of your clients or client groups? You might sell different products at different price points, so that the value varies according to the group. The important thing is that you do your homework and are absolutely sure of those numbers. Inside out, backwards and upside down. It will determine how much you can comfortably invest in keeping such valuable business.

How long term should your marketing plan be?

Most business owners plan for one year and possibly two, so in that case why not three? (More than three years is probably a little too far ahead.) Avoid cash flow problems by taking seasonal trends in sales activity into account and plan either to avoid low-revenue times or to reduce activity at these times to a minimum.

The length of your plan must suit your requirements. For example, if yours is a start-up business or if you are launching a new product, a big proportion of your marketing effort needs to be upfront. You will have to plan for establishing new brands and image creation, market research and competitor analysis. Moving into the second year, the emphasis might shift towards physical material, such as a printed brochure or catalogue and web presence. Come the third year and spend can be budgeted to drop, since by then you will have created a lot of material that can be reused in some way, updated and/or reprinted.

Once your plan has been running for a while, say a year, you can begin to assess what is working and what is not. You are likely to see where savings can be made as you forge relationships with your suppliers or try new ones. From year three onwards, excepting the need to support new products, you should see savings on the budget.

Measuring the results

Once your plan is under way, it is important to keep detailed records of spend, activity and results. This will help you with the future allocation of funds.

The kinds of marketing activities that you undertake will determine how you monitor and measure the return on your investment – it could be a system as simple as asking a new client how they found out about you by asking them to tick a box on a form. Whatever method you use, it is important that you do monitor the success rate of your marketing effort.

When a client calls your offices or makes contact with you for the first time, make sure that you ask them how they found your details, who referred you to them, where they saw your advert, from which magazine or web link they got your number, etc. This is hugely valuable in helping you know what is working best for you in reaching people. You can then look at the results and decide whether to repeat the activity the following year or to make some changes. As the business owner, you must have a clear understanding of the effectiveness of your marketing. After all, it's your money.

Controlling the marketing funds

From what I have observed of *Big Profit!* ventures, it is those where the budget is under the control of one person that enjoy the highest return on their marketing spend. People who want to draw from the funds have to submit carefully researched requests, backed up with documentation and an evaluation of the proposed return. They might be able to vote for their favourite proposal, but the final decision lies with the person in charge. Disagreements occur, but making staff members compete and justify their request for funds ensures the money is more likely to be well spent. If there is little control over the funds and anyone can dip in on an ad hoc basis, the money will soon disappear, probably with little to show for it.

Finding the hidden wealth in your business

Now that you have established when, where and on what you want to concentrate your marketing effort, you need to decide what it is about your business that you want to promote. Finding the hidden wealth is all about identifying your USPs, your unique selling propositions. What is it that is special about your offering that makes it different from the competition? Why do clients choose your product or service over any other? Is it to do with price, availability, ease of doing business with you, goodwill, speed of delivery, after-sales service, good credit terms, quality . . . ? Jot down all the reasons so that you are clear about them. If you are a sole operator, think of a USP as referring to you as a 'uniquely special person'.

Once your USPs are clear, you will be able to let people know who you are and why you are special, and therefore why people should trade with you rather than someone else. Business owners often market the concepts of quality, service and dependability. But no one buys these in isolation. You must express your USPs in ways that are both specific and measurable, highlighting to your clients the benefits that buying from you will bring to them.

Reputation is often cited as a reason for buying from a particular company, but remember that reputation is built on and is representative of something that a company does very well. It could be that it delivers a takeaway meal within thirty minutes of your placing your order. Or perhaps one of its taxis will collect you from your meeting within five minutes of receiving your call. How about the USP of the company that offers to supply you with a replacement laptop while yours is being repaired, or the small hotel that takes your booking for accommodation, offering a no-quibble money-back guarantee – and when you complain in the morning cheerfully cancels your booking fee? All of these are expressions of good service, but are simply defined within boundaries that allow both client and company to know when the company owes the client an apology and a free product or a refund.

How perceptive is your audience?

It is also worth stopping to think about how your clients might see you. Do you think they perceive your USPs in the same way as you do? If not, do you want to change the way they regard you? Or perhaps they are overlooking an important part of your offering? For example, when asked what business they are in, the typical responses of some business owners might be: 'I run a beauty salon', or 'I'm an interior designer', or 'I run a restaurant'. Yet if their clients were asked what the businesses delivers, they might respond with a different set of answers, such as:

- 'They help boost my confidence.'
- 'They make my house a beautiful and restful place.'
- 'They take the hassle and the stress out of entertaining at home.'

So marketing is not just a question of getting your message across to people, it can also address problems with the way people regard your business, or put the spotlight on certain areas. What benefits do you think your clients see in your offerings? Are they overlooking or undervaluing any part of it? (See also 'Freedom of choice' in Chapter 5.)

One way of finding out is to hold an **assessment** or **focus group** to determine how others see your product or service. Organized on a formal basis, this kind of market research is not cheap, so make sure that you think carefully about the questions you want asked and discuss them with the focus group organizer beforehand. You might ask: What is it about our offering that you like/don't like? What parts of our business are you aware of? How do you rate our business within the industry? Questions can be specific, to give you detailed feedback, or general to assess how aware people are of your presence. This will also soon give you a strong insight into the advantages for which people are willing to pay.

Remember, however, that focus groups are not 100% foolproof. The public can be fickle and might say one thing to a market researcher but do another in practice. (See also the section on client feedback in Chapter 7.)

Getting noticed – ways and means

There are a number of methods that you might consider in order to capture the attention of your clients and make sure that your marketing message gets noticed. Here are a few of them.

Sector-specific print media

Every industry, sub-branch and sector has its own associations. The majority of these still have print media for their readership, members, subscribers and clients. Print media means magazines, newsletters, periodicals, journals and regular updates sent by post. Advertising in these publications can be an effective way to reach business clients, but you will need to test them carefully to make sure they suit your requirements before agreeing to advertise in them long term, even if the hugely discounted price seems too good to pass up at the outset.

Group speaking engagements

Public speaking is a natural and very powerful marketing tool. Bearing in mind that many people find speaking in public intimidating, the very fact that you are doing so will create a good impression among many of your audience. By speaking knowledgeably about your area of expertise, the idea that you are well qualified to do business with them will be reinforced. Your audience will also have first-hand experience of you, making it easier for them to refer you on if you were previously unknown to them.

Many owners of *Big Profit!* ventures endorse this practice. Simply being in front of a group of people will win you business – and not just among members of the audience but by referrals from that audience within their own networks. You could potentially achieve far more by a talk or presentation to a group of just twenty people than you could ever hope to with twenty one-to-one meetings. You also save yourself a lot of time.

Dust down your ideas and brush up on your presentation skills and get out there. Make that group of strangers understand who you are and what your business can do for them. You might be surprised by the results.

You and your trading name

In marketing terms, removing your name from the brand could make a significant contribution. New clients searching the Internet or phone book for the kind of services or products you supply do so by category of service or product, not by name.

We learned this lesson quickly. The address of my first business website was my surname.com. This was fine for people who knew me already, or who met me at Chamber of Commerce events or industry shows, but lessened the chances of new clients finding me. When we bought some domain names that were more closely linked to the nature of our business, we saw a slight but steady increase in bookings and sales. The new domain names flagged up the nature of the business immediately.

Your organization is more than just your name, and is more likely to be identified with the quality of what you offer than who you are.

Other ideas to help publicize your business

- Client questionnaires or survey cards, and phone calls made to a cross-section of clients by a trained telephone canvasser seeking to raise specific questions. There always needs to be some incentive for the client to take part, such as entry in a prize draw, a discount voucher against a future purchase, or a free gift. These are all methods similar to those described in the section on client feedback in Chapter 7 (page 101), but they can be used to equally good effect in raising the profile of your business.
- The sponsoring and commissioning of industry surveys.
- Web-based downloads.
- Monthly email newsletter. This can go out to your existing clients, but with a note inviting them to forward it to any colleagues or acquain-

tances who might have an interest in the content. The newsletter should give the reader an option to subscribe or unsubscribe.

Creating your own publicity machine – getting yourself into print

1 **Establish your audience** – Who do you want to reach? Again it's a simple point, but one that is worth making as it is sometimes overlooked. Ordinary members of the public? If so, from what income group and social background? Other small businesses, large corporate outfits, public-sector bodies? Be specific.

2 **Learn their reading habits** – What do they *pay* to read? Notice that I did not simply say what do they read. When people pay to read certain publications it is because they are committed to knowing more about a subject. Clubs, institutes, associations, trade bodies, social organizations, professional interest groups, chambers of commerce, union organizations and education societies all have one thing in common – in-house magazines, newsletters and websites.

3 **Get yourself into print** – The editors of both printed and online publications are always keen to receive well-written articles and news items that they can use in their publications. If you can be relied upon to produce interesting copy on time, they will value your input. By getting yourself into print in these publications, you are raising your profile and establishing your expertise in front of the very audience to whom you wish to sell. And articles of this nature, that promote you as a by-product, will carry more credibility for your audience than printed advertising. Ask the publication to send you its media pack. It will contain contact names and possibly a list of topics to be addressed in the year ahead. Such advance information allows you to consider which topics you could write about and then to submit an idea for publication.

4 **Think long term** – The long-term *Big Profit!* opportunity is likely to be much more rewarding than any short-term cash benefits. If you are willing to provide a well-crafted piece about your topic, at no cost and written for the interest of your reader, an editor is more likely to allow you a tag line (one or two sentences about you at the end of the article, usu-

ally accompanied by a way that the reader can get in touch with you). Offer a free information sheet to readers as a further incentive for them to contact you. Simply having your website and phone number listed can be worth the equivalent of many thousands of pounds spent on advertising. If you insist on being paid for your piece, you are less likely to be allowed a tag line.

5 **Leverage the opportunity** – Once you have had articles published, you can send out copies with your usual sales or literature packs. This will enhance your standing in the eyes of the potential customers who receive them. They are far more likely to see you as the expert who will be able to help them. If you are giving a presentation to a number of people, you can hand out copies of your published articles instead of having to create new literature or adapt existing handouts for the occasion.

Making it easy for people to buy from you – taking away the risk

Attract clients to your venture by using marketing strategies that demonstrate that there is a tangible benefit from using your products or services. Put simply, this makes it easier for them to buy from you. What about attracting clients with an ethical bribe? You could offer to pay for the new software needed if a client decides to switch their account to you, or even pay them double for the inconvenience.

Both risk reversal and guarantees work well as marketing strategies that make buying from you an attractive proposition. Deliver successfully on them and you can build client relationships from which you attract referrals. Referrals will earn you good sales in less time and with lower costs than conventional marketing. In effect, your existing clients and contacts do your marketing for you.

Here are three ideas to make buying from you easier and therefore more attractive.

1. Risk reversal

When two parties enter into a transaction, one party always assumes more responsibility or liability in the deal than the other. A simple example is of a man who buys an MP3 player. The seller is responsible for supplying a player in good working order and probably with a guarantee for a specific period. The buyer hands over £150 of his hard-earned money in good faith. He has peace of mind thanks to the guarantee, although it is effective only for a certain period of time and will not cover breakage through misuse. The seller meanwhile knows that there is a low risk of the player breaking down during the period of the guarantee.

However, if the seller were to offer an extended guarantee free, thereby taking more of the risk upon himself, he would be making the deal more attractive to the buyer through risk reversal. Risk reversal is about making it so easy for the buyer that he feels that the possibility of any problems has been minimized or even removed completely.

Another example is a mail order company that doesn't cash clients' cheques or debit their credit cards until 30 days after the goods are shipped. Risk reversal behaviour as good as this is likely to increase the response rate to an advert making this kind of offer. So it could be worth formalizing such a procedure within your own business.

If your product or service is of quality and value, the likelihood of people exercising their right to a refund or needing to use an extended guarantee could be lower than you expect. Because so few businesses are willing to step up to the line and take the risk out of the transaction for the buyer, those who do can reap huge rewards.

A final word of caution. Clearly, your risk reversal offer needs to be carefully judged. You don't want to offer something that could backfire on you and actually lose you money, even if thousands of people buy from you as a result of it.

2. Guarantees

A guarantee ensures that when someone does business with you, you guarantee some part of the transaction to them. It could be that if your product breaks within 60 days of purchase, you will replace it immediately, no questions asked. Or perhaps that if they can find a cheaper equivalent elsewhere, you will refund the difference in price.

A guarantee gives the client peace of mind about certain aspects of the transaction and, in addition, they understand that you value their custom. You ensure that they get what they expect and thereby protect them from disappointment or loss.

The higher the guarantee you offer to your clients, the more they will buy. But you must deliver on your promises and be clear about any restrictions on the guarantee. If you use small print to try to wriggle out of some part of it, you will soon acquire a reputation for being a slippery operator.

3. Referrals and referral networks

Business arising from referrals is normally more profitable and has a sounder basis, being more likely to lead to a lasting new client relationship, than business arising from conventional advertising. The fact that a product or service has been recommended by a friend or acquaintance allows the buyer to feel safer and happier about requesting and accepting the seller's marketing. Since it is initiated by the client, such permission-based marketing creates a strong platform for referrals.

Four-step system to winning referral business

1 Remind clients of the value of your product or service and its impact on or benefit to your client.

2 Let them know that you feel your greatest contribution is doing more of what you do well and that you prefer to invest profits in the company rather than spend excessively on high-profile marketing campaigns.

3 Make sure that your clients are aware that they can benefit from referring people to you. Offer them free entry in a prize draw or a free gift if they recommend you.

4 Let clients know that you can refer or introduce them to other businesses who are ready to do business with them, or who could be influential on their behalf or introduce them to new contacts and new opportunities.

Here is an example of referral business in action.

CASE IN POINT

Jackson Michaels is a medium-size accountancy firm with around thirty staff. It specializes in preparing accounts and tax returns for small businesses (which it defines as companies with less than six staff).

One of the firm's account managers visited a craft shop and picked up half a dozen of the various business cards on display and began calling.

He was able to make appointments to visit the chairperson, the treasurer and the assistant chair of the guild, and as a result received introductions to six other guild members requiring accounting and bookkeeping services. Since then he has visited the shop twice more and gathered more leads. From just one of those

▶

businesses, the account manager gained contacts with a further seven artists exhibiting in a city-centre gallery.

And from one of the more active business owners (who understood the value of helping create new and expanding networks that would benefit them both), he was given an introduction to another craft group which comprised larger and more professional businesses such as furniture manufacturers and antiques dealers. This group has 40 member businesses, most of them employing several staff.

From that first visit to the craft shop, the account manager achieved a total of 31 referrals that required bookkeeping or accounting services. These translated into actual invoices each with a value of between £500 and £2,000.

Now think about your own business:

- How much do you invoice for your time or product?
- Therefore, how much is referral business worth to you?
- How many referrals are you getting? And how often?
- Finally, how can you improve on your rate of referrals?

If you are lucky enough to have too much referral business, can you cherry-pick to concentrate on the more profitable contracts, or even take on staff to handle the extra business?

Maintaining contact with your customers

This is crucial for many reasons. Some of your clients will only trust you if they know you are going to be around for a while. Many will not give you referrals until they have seen you several times or had several transactions with your business. It's all about building a relationship with them. This does not mean that you have to visit them at their premises each month in person, but it will help if you see them a couple of times a year at the **network events** that they attend.

Other ways of staying in contact are via a simple **email newsletter** that you can use to keep in touch with large numbers of people. This approach allows you to maintain relationships and keep a large number of people as warm leads with the minimum of effort. As you get to know individual clients better, you might want to cut out and send them **articles from magazines, industry journals and local newspapers** that you know would be of interest to them. Don't be afraid to ask them for a couple of back issues of their own industry magazine. (See also Chapters 4 and 7 for additional advice on staying in touch with clients and good communication.)

CHAPTER NINE

Growth and future direction

Moving forward

Having got this far – both with your *Small Business, Big Profit!* venture and with the book – your eyes will be focused firmly on the horizon. After all the time and effort that you have invested in your future, not to mention the money, it is important to have a clear view of where you are going.

If you are still a one-person venture or run a home-based business with a partner, you might feel that the time is now right to bring on board some new people and to begin delegating some of your workload. Alternatively, if you already have a number of staff on the payroll, you might have moved beyond this point, but feel that there are still aspects of your business which could be developed further. Once you have reached this stage, making the leap to being the proud employer of your first ten or twelve staff is soon achieved.

But, let's get back to an important question, one that I have raised a few times already during the course of this book: What are you in this for? For your own sake and for that of your staff, as your business grows, you must have the answer to this question at the forefront of your mind.

Will you carry on as you are, making a profit after overheads and taxes, and view the business as a lucrative (I hope) job alternative? Or will you look for a potential buyer for the business? What about adding another aspect to it by buying an outfit that has some synergy with your own activities but which reaches a different audience? There would be some natural gains to be had from such a link.

At this stage you have three main options:

1 To stay as you are, trading profitably with no intention to change.
2 To sell the business for a profit and focus on some new challenges.
3 To grow and expand the business through acquisition and development.

Staying as you are

Staying as you are doesn't mean struggling for existence – I hope this book has shown you how you can run a profitable but small enterprise; rather, it's a positive choice to keep your business, and keep it at a size that is manageable for you.

Selling the business

Business owners decide to sell up for a number of reasons. Sometimes purely for the money, but sometimes for reasons such as stepping down to let other family members take over the reins, or to allow a management buyout by the existing partners or staff. Alternatively, sometimes one part of a business is sold off in order to provide the funds to develop another. Businesses are also sold to enable the founder to release his or her capital (hopefully now healthily augmented after being tied up in the venture) in order to pursue other business or personal activities.

Regardless of your motives for selling, it is crucial that you think through the process carefully. The success of a disposal can easily be placed in jeopardy simply by failing to maximize the opportunities for the sale. Once the deal is done and your business has gone, that's it. No amount of wishful thinking or the wisdom of hindsight can put the clock back if you don't feel the deal you have struck is going to bring you the maximum benefits.

So, this can be a toughie! You have spent years watching over and nurturing your business. It's become your child; it's part of you. How could you sell it and simply walk away? Don't you care any more?

Seriously though, what do you want to do? To be sure of your answer, you must return to your guiding principles and your motivation for being in business, as discussed in Chapters 1 and 2. Do you want to sell so that you can devote more time to your family? Is it time to explore other avenues of activity? Do you want to realize some hard cash from the *Big Profits!* that you have built up? Perhaps you want to sell just a portion of the business in order to inject some cash into the rest of the operation? If so, how will you cope with the reduced amount of control that will be the inevitable result of such a course of action?

CASE IN POINT

Recently, I spent a day with a client who, over twenty years, has built up a thriving print business. He has 26 staff and retains around £400,000 after tax each year on a turnover of £2 million. He has bought his factory premises outright at a cost of around £1.1 million. His goal is to use the money from the sale of his business (around £1.5million) and the £120,000 yearly rent that he will charge on the factory premises to fund his family's move to Mexico. His eldest daughter will be ready to attend university in a couple of years' time and the whole family speak Spanish fluently.

So far, so good. The business owner has prepared very thoroughly for the financial and logistical aspects of the sale and is ready to register with a business sale broker. However, now that everything is in place, his thoughts are turning inwards, towards the effect the sale will have on him emotionally. Twenty years is a long time to be your own master. His original plan was to secure a deal where he would be retained as a consultant, advising from his new base in Mexico and attending board meetings on trips back to the UK. But he is beginning to realize that, for him personally, this would be one bridge too far. To still be involved and yet not be in complete control would just be too frustrating and dissatisfying. A clean break is what is required, leaving him free to concentrate on pursuing new activities and enjoying the income from the factory premises and other properties he owns.

Selling the business is likely to be a roller-coaster ride of mixed emotions. Sometimes you are up, relishing the prospect of the financial outcome, and at others you are down, wondering if you are doing the right thing. On the one hand you fear having to relinquish the control that you have exerted for so long, and on the other you feel great pride at having built up the business to the point that it can now be sold as a profitable concern.

Can your business stand on its own two feet?

Getting the correct valuation for your *Small Business, Big Profit!* venture is as much a question of getting the timing right as anything else. If you have developed a 'turnkey operation' which will enable your buyer to walk straight into a going concern that is no longer dependent upon your own personal style of running the show, then you will get a maximum price.

If you are not at the turnkey stage yet, but at least having begun to implement some of the SSP technologies discussed in Chapter 4 you have reached the point where these systems can be developed further, this will be a good place to start. However, if your business could not cope during your absence, even just for a two-week holiday, then think again. In such a set-up, the chances of finding anyone that might be prepared to invest in your company, let alone an outright buyer, are extremely slim.

Selling up – key pointers

1. Make sure the reason why you are selling is clear

Buyers want to know that you are selling and that they are buying a business for all the right reasons. Don't allow doubts as to your motives for selling to creep into your buyers' minds. Make it clear that the business has been a good vehicle for you and therefore that there is every reason to believe that it will be a good vehicle for them too.

2. Don't make your intention to sell known until you are ready

This may seem like common sense, but common sense is not common! Work on the operational and financial aspects of your venture as if preparing them for a private audit, but without allowing potential buyers to become aware of this. Rumour of an impending sale or too much advance information can have a negative impact on a successful outcome. Only make your intention to sell known when the documentation is complete and you are ready.

3. Get the timing right

Is your industry enjoying a current growth curve? Are you still regarded as a hot and desirable property in a rising sector? Or perhaps new product innovation shows clearly that there are untapped revenues still there for the taking? Timing the sale correctly will also ensure that your buyer will recognize the value of your business and see the potential for increasing it. So, make sure that you are selling while there is still some *Big Profit!* left for the next owner to make.

4. Would someone want to buy your business today?

 If the answer is not an immediate yes, then you have some work to do. But simply by asking yourself this question, you give yourself the opportunity to develop the business into a valuable commodity for sale. Go back to basics and review your SSP technologies. What tasks could your least-qualified employees take on if you were to introduce an operations manual or process folder? Should you review your buying procedures in order to reduce costs? Could your pricing model be assessed to look for margin enhancements on sales? Is it time you examined your client data to see if you are missing potential opportunities for promoting existing and new products?

5. Create a timetable for the sale

Knowing when you want to sell enables you to assess what improvements need to be made and by when. Do you need to improve upon payments to creditors? Are the correct staff in place? Perhaps there are staff members you hope to retain and whose presence in the company at the time of sale would be a positive asset, while there may be others whom you would like to lose. Work with your advisers to make sure that, if it is not already in place, the accounting documentation that will be required for the sale is assembled in good time. Ironically, in a business that is being retained there is a natural tendency to maintain the lowest tax position possible. This contrasts with a business that is to be sold, where profits need to be seen to be healthy, although, unfortunately, healthy profits also attract a similarly robust tax bill.

6. Work out your sales price parameters

You need to have two figures in mind when you put your business up for sale. One will be the optimum price, the one you would like to achieve, and the other the worst-case scenario, the one you can live with if you have to. The lowest figure will be the one that that you calculate you can accept while making you a profit and justify the effort of having groomed the business for sale. The optimum price will be based on various different valuation approaches (see box) and will leave you with a healthy profit.

Methods of valuing a business

Asset valuation – A price based on the total value of all assets, both tangible and intangible, held by the business (includes cash, property, intellectual property, brands, stock, etc.).

Discounted cash flow – This looks at the return on investment received on the cash a buyer uses to acquire your business, compared with how that same money might have been used elsewhere within the buyer's existing business.

Earnings multiple – The last full tax year's earnings multiplied by the factor used within your industry to determine the value of the business.

Market benchmarks – A comparative method that looks at the prices achieved in the sale of a similar or related business within your industry.

Return on investment – This uses a price (of sale) / annual earnings ratio that indicates the number of years required for the business to have paid off its purchase price.

Sector valuation – This is where a valuation is reached by using the average performance within the industry sector as a yardstick (for example, the annual fee income from a consultancy, the number of bed spaces sold by a hotel group per year, the subscription income from a mail order business, the land bank reserves held by a builder, the annual spend per name on your database, etc.).

---

7. Involve staff and keep them informed

There is nothing like the prospective sale of a business to worry staff at all levels. And, if managed badly, the doubt and uncertainty that a sale spawns can cause resignations just when you least want them. On the other hand, keeping people fully informed and involving key staff can aid preparation for the sale significantly. If staff know there is a role for them in the ongoing organization they will be more willing to work with you on the improvements that need to be made.

Before the sale, buyers will want to find out about the strengths of the team they are taking over and how they can make best use of individual team members' abilities. Providing buyers with an insight into your staff's strengths and skills is a good way of helping you to be more involved with ensuring that loyal staff are rewarded with good positions in the new venture. Saying goodbye to your employees and wondering how they will fare under the new owner is perhaps the most difficult issue in selling a business. However, if they are able workers and have proved themselves reliable and conscientious, they should be in a strong position.

8. Non-competition agreements

A non-competition agreement in which you agree that you will not compete with the business you are selling is a common requirement, so be prepared for this. It could be on the basis of a geographical limitation, or a period of time during which you are contractually bound not to operate a similar or related venture in competition with your buyer.

Growing through acquisition and development

To make your company a more attractive proposition for an outright sale at some time in the future, you might wish to look at developing it further or acquiring another venture. Acquisition is generally most advantageous for the buyer, who will often be picking up a small outfit with just a handful of staff. Such small set-ups are frequently bought for the value of their client databases, rather than the company's employees.

This immediately raises the thorny question of whether those employees should be retained. To take them all on to your existing payroll might mean some duplication of roles, despite the fact that some of the staff might have built up good relationships with the client group. On the other hand, you might be buying a business that will sit quite happily as an independent venture alongside your existing business, operating smoothly with very little change needing to be made.

In either situation, one of your most difficult tasks will be integrating the culture and systems of the new business with those of your own. Not surprisingly, venture capitalists frequently highlight the integration of different cultures as a potential problem. And what happens if some staff from the company you are acquiring decide to leave, just when you need them to bring you up to speed with their systems? And how does your team react if you appoint a person from the acquired venture to a position of greater responsibility in the newly created larger structure? What effect would this have on the motivation and morale of your existing team?

Still, despite the fact that integrating two companies is not easy, it will probably not be enough to scare you away from a highly lucrative deal. After all, you are an entrepreneur and you thrive upon the excitement of the chase and relish the prospect of the benefits such a deal could bring.

Finding the right acquisition

If you decide to try the acquisition route, it is almost inevitable that at some stage you will come across a venture that looks undervalued when such assets as its intellectual property, client database, annual subscription revenues, etc., are taken into account.

Companies that grow fast often do so by acquiring other businesses, in pursuit of the new company's assets or databases but frequently overlooking their human resources.

When you acquire a new company, review the staff, obtaining first the departing owner's opinion of them, but also making a point to talk to each staff member individually yourself. Failure to recognize and value the skills of the staff who have been acquired will soon result in a brain drain of talent, almost certainly within the first year of the takeover. Reassure the staff and make sure you show your appreciation early on, before it is too late. Once you have lost them, you may begin to realize just how much they contributed to the company if its performance decreases and results start to take a downward turn. A sure way of chasing away the people that you really want to keep is to place one of your own managers in charge of them, who will insist rigidly that 'this is how we do things'.

It is often the case that it is the most proactive staff who decide to leave at the time of acquisition. Those who depart may prove to have been the best and the brightest of the bunch, leaving behind those who are too timid to make the break. These people can be a huge drain on your resources if they cling to the past, dwelling on issues that are no longer relevant under the new regime, or resenting and reacting badly to the changes that you want to make.

But – and this is a big but – don't dismiss out of hand those staff who are left. There could be some real stars among them. They might have felt stifled and unable to reach their full potential under the previous management. Give them the chance to see that things could be different and give them an opportunity to come forward with their ideas. You could both benefit – you from their innovative ideas and the staff from increased morale at being able to contribute and feeling appreciated.

Make the most of the opportunities for change and growth that the acquisition of another venture creates. But beware of overadministrating or trying to exert too much control, which could stifle the potential of some staff. Keep an eye out also for bullying tactics from any staff members frightened of losing their positions of authority. Make a point to seek out any such individuals and ensure they are pruned from the organization.

Growing through development

Being able to embrace and encourage change is fundamental to the growth of your *Small Business, Big Profit!* venture. How change is brought about is not the main issue – it could be through new systems, or the acquisition or disposal of a company, or even just through the humble suggestion box in the staff coffee room. Your ability to create new ideas yourself and foster a culture in which suggestions and innovation from the staff are encouraged, will contribute greatly to your overall success.

CASE IN POINT

There is one particular group of people with whom I have worked who impressed me greatly with their ability to adapt to changing market forces and circumstances. I'm not talking about one of the manufacturing or service industries, or even the property sector, but rather the farming industry. Whether fighting the effects of cattle disease, crop failure and the ravages of nature, or coping with fluctuations in market prices and the power of the supermarkets, they have grasped the importance of a realistic and flexible approach.

I don't wish to suggest that you become a farmer. The hours alone could kill you if you are not used to them! But I am suggesting that you draw inspiration from how other individuals and industries remain open to change, enabling them to adapt to different circumstances when necessary. Think about the way you normally respond to certain situations. Perhaps you should be reacting differently?

If your business is practical in nature (perhaps you supply food to restaurants or erect fences and lay paving), that should not preclude you from exploring alternative income streams, such as the possibility of developing income from intellectual property. And of course, conversely, if you deal in intellectual property, don't overlook any chances to develop any more practical sidelines. Keep a lookout for any different products that could be sold to your existing client group and keep yourself informed about your industry market in general.

It is not true to say that all innovation will be positive. It is quite likely that only a few of the new ideas that you try will work and that only some of the new products you launch will be profitable. But, nothing ventured, nothing gained. If you don't discuss new ideas internally, sound out your clients for feedback on them and provide revenue for them to be tested, you will never know what could have been. And just because an idea does not work in one sector of your business does not mean that it will fail in another. But even if an idea does not work out, you can still draw something positive from the experience by learning what not to do in the future, or how something can be improved upon. Without change your business will stagnate and become paralyzed, caught in the gaze of a predator who has spotted the *Small Business, Big Profit!* potential which you have been too blind to see or too timid to explore. And you wouldn't want that to happen, would you?

So, are you providing an environment for change?

- Do employees feel able to approach you with a new idea? Are you prepared to discuss new ideas and do you have the space and resources for feasibility testing?
- When a client complains, do you as the business owner deal with it, or is it dealt with by a member of staff much lower down the chain?
- Are you comfortable with allowing someone else to be in control of a project or an initiative?
- If a competitor starts to win some of your market share, how soon do you get to know about it?
- Do you have systems, strategies and processes in place that are giving strength and value to the business?
- Who or what stands in the way of your business being more successful?
- Do you get approached by job seekers because your business has a reputation for being a place that embraces change and where profits are created from innovation?
- Are you able to let go sufficiently in order to delegate and allow others to assume important roles so that growth can happen *organically?*

Good luck in all that you do. Let us know of your successes and failures and what you learn from them.

Index